PERFORMING
AS
YOU

How to have authentic impact
in every role you play

**DIANA
THEODORES**

RETHINK PRESS

First published in Great Britain in 2019 by Rethink Press
(www.rethinkpress.com)

Praise

'It is one thing to be able to engage in person and quite another on paper...This is an amazing book! The way Diana weaves together her advice with personal memories, clients, stories and inspiring quotes from role models, plays and poetry makes this such an easy and exciting read.
This is business story telling at its best!'

– Susan Vinnicombe CBE, Professor of Women and Leadership, Cranfield University

'Diana's gifts helped me take my speaking and leadership to a fuller level of expression. I never thought she could capture her magic in a book... and she did it! This book is so timely as courageous authenticity is needed more than ever.'

– Johanne Lavoie, co-author of *Centered Leadership: Leading with Purpose, Clarity, and Impact* and McKinsey & Company Partner

'This book is *the* toolkit to direct your own career, an inspirational read!'

– Autumn Le Fevre, Head of Regulatory Compliance, HSBC Luxembourg

'This book radically changed the way I think about work and the impact I can have.'

– Sarah Fennell, Diversity & Inclusion Lead, EMEA, Moody's Corporation

'Engaging and emotive book about being authentically yourself – highly recommended!'

– Josefin Holmberg, Partner, True Search

'These words of wisdom and exercises helped me to build my confidence and self-belief to be at my best.'

– Kate Jones, Partnership Development Manager, Mercedes F1 Team

'A practical, uplifting, life-affirming book to help you shine.'

– Jo Palmer, Director Divestment, Development & Group Property, Lloyds Banking Group

'This book is a gift that helps me to be more effective every day. I feel stronger already!'

– Julianne Antrobus, Director of Products & Technology, Global Nuclear, SNC Lavalin Atkins

'What was I scared of? Diana Theodores is the coach you want in your pocket. This book is a game changer.'

– Sarah Rayner, Senior Director of Operations and Culture, EDITION

For my mother, Rose, who
was my champion and challenger

Contents

Introduction

Imagine if the 'you' in your workplace and the 'you' in your life outside those doors got together and became soulmates. Imagine that 'lifework' was a real word and it meant 'the connection between your work life and your outside life'. Imagine what a favour you'd be doing your organisation if the 'outside' you made more than an occasional guest appearance and showed up a *lot* more. How vivid and inspiring the world of work would be if you dared to be a bit more *you!*

Performing as you harnesses your life force: your experience and wisdom, your talents and gifts – the ones you acknowledge and use and the ones that are waiting to reawaken; it harnesses those moments when you feel in your element, and when you've exercised resilience and courage; it harnesses your creative energy and the sources of your inspiration.

It takes awareness and some practice, but you already have everything you need to perform as *you* and enjoy the liberating and lucrative results. All you need is to *give yourself permission* to bring more of you to the table. This book shows you how to do just that.

What is this book?

Think of me as the 'coach in your pocket': I'll prep you and get you focused. I'll free you up to be more authentic, more confident and more credible. I'll help calm and centre you when you're feeling under stress. I'll challenge the stories that no longer serve you and help you craft new ones that are much more accurate and potent. I'll remind you to reflect and restore in order to perform at your best. I'll help keep you receptive, responsive and alert to your wonderful aliveness. I'll help you get unstuck when you forget that you have choices for impact beyond those in your default zone. I'll liberate your voice for more effective expression. I'll support you in manifesting your vision, and I'll be a mirror to reflect your strengths and unique gifts. I hope you feel a big heart coming at you to fortify, support, nudge, challenge and applaud you as you step into your fullest self and shine in every role you play.

Here's the deal – this is what you'll get:

1. **Reassurance** – through stories that demonstrate you are not alone in your challenges

2. **Evidence** – of transformative results via client case studies

3. **Pointers and perspectives** – that liberate you from limiting habits and beliefs

4. **Inspiration** – to reclaim your creative powers and upgrade your impact

5. **Dynamic tools** – for fuller presence and engagement in all your environments

6. **An irresistible invitation** – to ignite your fire, grow your wings and lift off into your best personal performance

Who do I think I am?

Growing up in New York, I was nourished on a diet of great performances. From Bernstein to Baryshnikov to Broadway, these performances ignited and inspired me so much that I entered the world of dance and theatre and spent years directing artists to perform brilliantly. Now I'm a performance coach on the business stage. Performance is not just in the domain of the arts. We are all performers, and everyone wants to perform their best in life. All the world *is* a stage, and the greatest role you ever get to play is that of *you*. When you perform as you, you connect first to yourself, deeply and truthfully, and then to the world.

Over the last decade I've coached thousands of wonderful, smart, talented women just like you. From that intimate, privileged vantage point I've witnessed your humanity, your gifts and your transformative 'aha' moments. Maybe I've worked with you in person, but chances are I haven't had the pleasure of working with you, and that's the reason I wrote this book. I'd like to reach you. I'm on your side. I want you to move yourself forward to enjoy greater performance, fulfilment and service – for you, your organisation and your life.

Why am I talking to women in particular?

Being and bringing more of ourselves through the door is a challenge, a quest and a joy for both men and women, and everything in this book will most certainly resonate with men too. (Men, you are hereby invited to read this book!) But I have put women centre stage in writing this because their 'me time' is at such a premium, because they can sometimes be hard of hearing when it comes to messages of self-permission – so this book dials it up good and loud – and because, let's face it, there's a bigger history of male templates around leading and influencing, and women could do with a bit of template-crafting of their own.

Contradictions, politics and ever-changing perspectives on gender equality and the advancing of female talent abound, from Sheryl Sandberg's *Lean In* to Michelle Obama's 'It's a lie, you can't have it all'. Nevertheless, there are some consistent realities for women: the aspiration for fulfilment in work, the ambition for personal and professional growth, and the economic necessity of single-working-woman and single-working-mother households as well as two-earner households.

Wherever you are on this spectrum, I hope we can agree that organisations and their cultures can be healthier, happier and more sustainable if the people in them feel supported, valued and purposeful. It would help to have a lot more women as players in this enlightened leadership field. We need their voices and visibility to manifest this story. But that on its own is not enough. Women could also use some space to build a bit more muscle. Here's what I mean.

When I was thirteen, I decided I wanted to be a ballerina. At that age, I was already late to the party for becoming a professional dancer, as there was a lot of technique to acquire. I remember seeing boys who were considerably older but got promoted in performances much sooner. They caught up faster. Why? Because they had a muscular head start. They didn't have to build muscle strength so much as refine that strength into expressive technique.

My thirteen-year-old fury went something like this: 'They waltz in here and get all the attention just because they can lift us up!' In the ballet world, boys had more muscle so they did the lifting, and in those days they also did most of the choreographing.

I love coaching men as well as women, and of course *men will benefit from this book too*! But, like dancers, women need to build some muscle so they can focus on *how* they want to express themselves authentically in the roles they play. This book offers women especially a 'rehearsal space' where that can happen.

CHAPTER 1

Your Body Is Your First Environment

*What makes a fire burn
is space between the logs,
a breathing space.*[1]

JUDY BROWN

Connect to yourself before you connect to the world

You wake up and it all begins (OK, maybe you hit the snooze button a few times). Whether you're flying solo or you're getting the kids off to school, your day begins like the clapboard on a film set: 'And... action!'

You arrive at the office and before you've even removed your coat, you've opened your email and hastily rattled off a reply. You manage to get your coat off before making a call and then rush to your first meeting of the day. On the way, you're ambushed in the corridor by a colleague, a direct report or a boss who needs an immediate decision.

You buy some time, promising to come back to her later, and make a mental note to fit it in somewhere (meaning lunch will be a quick sandwich at your desk). Coming out of the meeting, you're not sure what it accomplished. And so your day goes, juggling requests, making or delaying decisions, rushing to meetings, presenting, pitching, phone conferencing, firefighting, *doing, doing, doing*. Faster and faster you go, often feeling on the back foot or hanging on for dear life, in a state of distraction and partial – continual – attention, autopilot or worse: survival mode.

Phew!

It doesn't have to be this way. With one simple practice, you can take hold of that clapboard and be in charge of when to call 'Action!' Drumroll please.

Take a moment. *Stop! and breathe.*

Tuning in to your breathing is so powerful and so critical for self-mastery that I'm going to coach you in it in various ways throughout this chapter.

In all that you do, in all your environments, your 'first environment' is your body, the source of balance in all the flux and complexity. Connecting to yourself before stepping into action is key to your well-being and therefore key to your performance. You may play many different roles in your work, but you have only one body, and it's the gateway to all your experience.

Your mindset, your power, your beliefs, your decision-making, your risk-taking, your acts of courage, your vision, your presence – this extraordinary palette of expression of *you* – is located in your body. In the words of Somatic Master Practitioner Jennifer Cohen, 'We don't have a body, we are a body.'[2]

The more you take the time to listen to your body, the more you can maintain your centre, feel present and be agile, moment to moment, in different scenarios. Ever notice what's happening in your body when you feel under pressure? Perhaps your jaw clenches, your shoulders tense or your arms cross tightly when you feel defensive or resistant. Perhaps you slump or lean to one side when you feel defeated, bored or resigned. Whatever the challenge or pressure you're feeling, your body itself takes on an attitude. It is speaking to you! When you notice it, you can shift it and feel the difference immediately. One small moment of physical awareness and response can shift you into a much more effective state.

Let's pause and do a quick body audit. Notice how you are right now in reading or listening mode – how you are sitting or standing; how you are breathing. Notice any tension or holding. Take your time. Now press the refresh button by taking a breath and making a change in your posture.

How can you possibly connect with the world – the external environments and the people in them – before you've connected with the immediate environment of *you*? Here's a mantra I want you to make your best friend:

Stop. Breathe. Take a moment. Connect.

I can't count the number of times I've heard people say, 'I never stop for me' or 'Stopping feels like an indulgence or guilty pleasure' or 'I need to be seen to be working' or 'I need to justify what they're paying me'. Hmmm, very interesting. Can you imagine an athlete getting fired because she maintained her fitness?

You're a performer, an athlete, too! As Jim Loehr said, you're a corporate athlete and your fitness and well-being are critical to your performance.[3] So please connect to your body, listen to your body and take care of your body. You can do this the easy way or the hard way: you can choose, starting right now, to

Stop! and breathe, to take a moment to get clear and connected, and to go *towards your agendas with intention*. Or you can continue to rush past, rush over or rush headlong through your days as one meeting leaks into another, draining your energy and back-footing your effectiveness. Enough said.

The tour de force of breathing

A few years ago, a CEO in the cosmetics industry invited me to design a training programme. In our first face-to-face meeting, the CEO dove straight into the agenda, talking at breakneck speed, dispensing with the meet-and-greet moment and scarcely taking the time to draw breath.

As she glanced through the headlines of my programme proposal, she took her first and only pause when she read the words 'Breath Work', to which she responded, without missing a beat or taking a breath, 'I've done breathing!' Onwards she raced. I referred her to another coach and can only hope they lived happily ever after and everyone stopped for breath from time to time!

Effective breathing is the holy grail of gravitas. Changing the way we breathe changes the way we feel, and therefore it has an impact on us and on all those around us. What does it mean to breathe? The breath is our beginning. Breath is our life story. We journey from our first breath to our last.

We often hold our breath in tension and we often breathe up high in the chest. By taking a deep breath, you create space inside yourself. In this fast world, a world that is always calling you *outwards*, stopping to breathe is your pathway *inwards*. The simple act of *stopping and breathing* gives you many gifts:

- It keeps you grounded and balanced

- It gives you ballast, that sure-footedness of being connected to the earth

- It clears your mind and sharpens your focus

- It primes you for acting with *intention* rather than reacting in a hurry

- It helps you to be more resilient – to get back to your centre more quickly whenever you get knocked off it

BREATHING EXERCISES

To make breathing your ally, try these simple exercises:

- ◉ Sit or stand comfortably. Imagine you're blowing up a balloon. Take a deep breath in and exhale in hard, short bursts to pump up that balloon. Give it one last burst of breath before 'tying the knot'. Notice how warmed up you feel from the exertion of breathing.

⊕ Sit or stand comfortably. Hold one finger in front of your face, arm's length away. Imagine your finger is a candle flickering on a dinner table (yes, think romantic dinner). Take a deep breath and exhale very slowly, controlling your airflow so that the candle flickers in the gentle breeze but never blows out. Notice how calm and relaxed you feel.[4]

⊕ Sit or lie down. Just for one moment enjoy the quiet. Just for one moment let go and enjoy the stillness. Just for one moment marvel at the miracle of your breath, which fuels your life force. Imagine that you are breathing into a landscape that you love, such as the mountains or the ocean, a meadow or lush woods, a vast desert. Literally feel yourself expanding as your breath reaches into the landscape.

Remember to *Stop! and breathe* before you make that important call, log on to your emails, launch into your day or jump into that meeting. *Stop! and breathe* when speaking and presenting, and before answering questions. This practice literally puts air and space around your thoughts and words. It helps you to act with intention.

You become what you practise. The executives I know who don't practise *Stop! and breathe* say it's because they don't have time. The ones who do practise report that they are more tuned in, more focused, and better managers of themselves, especially under pressure.

Creating your own ritual really helps. One client puts on headphones so that anyone passing by her office will assume she's on a call and won't interrupt her. The act of donning the headphones is also her reminder to herself to take that moment. Another client does a short visualisation of her favourite landscape, where she feels complete well-being, and another does a gratitude moment.

Do whatever it takes, but do take a moment to connect to you! The critical piece here is ritualising: consciously, systematically and on purpose.

The fear of breathing

In a corporate training room in London, an inspiring space with lots of natural light, creative décor, and room to move around in, twenty-five magnificent women came to the end of an off-site leadership programme and were about to re-enter their 'real' worlds again.

We'd done wild-card icebreakers to uproarious laughter, and high-energy warm-ups. We'd shared stories, challenges and action plans. To wrap up the day, we stood in a circle for what I call a 'valuing ritual'. It consisted of taking some deep, slow breaths with our hands on our hearts and taking a moment to appreciate the day, one another and ourselves.

As I looked at this room full of women standing in their full integrity and dignity, breathing in some self-acknowledgement, I saw many eyes welling up with tears and faces holding tight against the dam of emotion wanting to spring forth.

Breathing is our great tour de force of being. Breathing makes us possible and fuels our presence, energy, voice, thinking and feeling. *It beckons our feelings*, and that's why there wasn't a dry eye in the house.

In the rush, in the action-driven day-to-day of life, particularly corporate life, our breathing can become superficial and thin. This is what produces speech that is monotone and too fast. The deeper we breathe, the more we have to slow down. The more we slow down, the more present we are to sensation, to the moment and to feelings. Our broken hearts, elations, loves, losses, fears, dreams, courage, failures, triumphs – our very life stories – are written on the breath. When we breathe deeply, literally taking our breathing to heart, we honour ourselves.

So here's to the welling up of eyes, the flow of tears, and nervous laughter. Fear not. Touching that core of vulnerability for a moment through the power of breathing doesn't mean you'll have a meltdown at the office or be too emotional in your next presentation (genuine fears often expressed). It just means that you have a powerful resource whenever you want it; a way to value yourself and give the gift of compassion to yourself and to others. To quote Walt Whitman, 'I am larger, better than I thought... I did not know I held so much goodness.'[5]

Be self-centred

When we are centred, we are aligned and in balance. We are connected to the ground, to our roots – metaphorically and practically. Centring means getting balanced and feeling our equilibrium. When we are centred, we are open, upright and strong. We feel connected to the space and those around us. We have an expansive radar. We are poised for action.

Right before leaping, dancers drop down deep into a position called *plié*. They get fuelled for takeoff by going to a place of deep self-centring. Think about what getting self-centred means to you. We often mistake 'stepping back' or going to ground as a retreat, a stepping away from something. But in fact, this moment of centring is a powerful gathering of inner resources and connection. Like taking a moment to *Stop! and breathe*, getting self-centred and finding your balance, *your ballast*, will give you more choices for impact and how you respond in the moment.

Eden, a young executive in a global management consultancy firm, described her recurring experiences of 'difficult conversations' with colleagues and stakeholders. As she talked about feeling overlooked, undervalued and undermined, her language was filled with phrases like 'under attack' and 'feeling defeated', terms of embattlement and defence. She regretted that she didn't stand her ground or have the 'right' response in the moment. Furthermore, she shared her fears about not knowing all the answers in Q&A moments and of being found out (that old impostor syndrome tale).

I asked her about people she admired, who demonstrated the kind of behaviour she was striving for. She replied, 'People who look relaxed and settled in their own skin, who have the sense that they are on their own ground.' And the biggest revelation of all: she admired those who demonstrated that *knowing all the answers isn't as critical as engaging with the questions!*

By focusing on her state and getting centred before important conversations, Eden was able to engage more effectively and feel more 'at home' in herself. The self-centre is that place from which, feeling aligned and in balance, settled and alert, open and strong, you can 'go forth'.

Move!

Watch conductors or great speakers to see how much value is added when you engage your body as much as your mind. As writer and artist Austin Kleon puts it,

> 'You don't need a scientific study to tell you that sitting in front of a computer all day is killing you, and killing your work. We need to move, to feel like we're making something with our bodies, not just our heads. Work that comes from the head isn't any good.'[6]

Recently, during a women's leadership programme, my colleagues and I wanted to revise one of the sessions we'd planned. As we gathered together over the coffee break, we felt stuck, time pressured and less than our creative best. Suddenly someone blurted out, 'When in doubt, dance it out!' We all laughed and then spontaneously started dancing. Crazy as it sounds, we got unstuck and came up with a great new idea for the next session to further enliven the learning.

Later that day, after our roomful of fabulous women leaders had worked on strategic career planning, delved into organisational politics and discussed unconscious bias, it was time for an energy booster and a recharge – so we danced! The room was charged with laughter, light and energy. It was breathtakingly beautiful to witness. The women behind the job titles were wholly in their bodies, untethered from self-limiting barriers. As they danced, they were at once grounded and liberated, joyful and commanding, connected and inclusive, playful and purposeful.

Moving opens us up and brings a more animated self forward; something more truthful is revealed. It releases us physically, vocally, emotionally and energetically. This means literally moving in the space, getting physically warmed up, stretching, gesturing, lifting our posture up, opening our mouths, voices, eyes, faces and hearts.

Your open, uplifted body shifts your feeling state and injects you with positive energy. You are in the act of *warming up to yourself*. It can take you instantly from a tentative, apologetic, defensive or anxious state to a confident, energised and optimistic state. As social scientist Amy Cuddy says, 'Our bodies change our minds and our minds can change our behaviour, and our behaviour can change our outcomes.'[7]

So get moving. Here's to your next dance class, run or – just for a minute – going wild to some music. Close the door and let rip!

Your energy is your 'response-ability'

Claire, a director in the oil industry, told me about a meeting she had at regular intervals with her counterpart from another global hub. She described these meetings as 'all agenda and no engagement'. Claire explained how disappointed and frustrated she felt coming away from these meetings for their lack of connection, thinking time and dialogue.

As she described it, they would barely get seated and settled before her counterpart would thrust out the agenda, summarise the objective of the meeting and proceed to race through the bullet points with barely a look up. There was no preliminary human moment, no literal or metaphorical meet-and-greet and no pause for reflection, second thoughts or questions. There was a hard stop and a rush out the door at the meeting's end. Needless to say, Claire developed an aversion to these meetings. They left her feeling unseen and unheard.

This is an extreme example but similar 'bottom-line-behaviour', focused entirely on outcomes and very little on the process, frequently arises in numerous workplaces. Team leaders, bosses and colleagues rush past and over the human moments. They fail to make a connection and be present. People default to this pattern for many reasons, such as insecurity in their position, terror of not knowing the answers (so they avoid making space for questions), wanting to be seen as time efficient and so on. What's clear is that there's a complete neglect of the *Stop! and breathe* moment, which should be minimal preparation for entering into a meeting environment with others. There also isn't any calibrating of energy, nor getting centred enough to be fully present.

Amy, from a global tech company, had a very different experience. Amy was asked by her boss to make a key presentation to the board, an indication of the investment in her future. On the big day, Amy rushed to the boardroom, hardly breathing, heart pounding, eyes fixed forward in tunnel-vision mode – a woman on a mission! Suddenly, her boss appeared in the corridor and stopped her in her tracks. Embarrassed and flustered, Amy heard her boss say, 'Slow down, or you'll take that nervous energy into the room with you.' Amy said it was the best feedback she ever got.

Your energy awareness and energy tuning is your responsibility. You can help create an environment where people listen, engage and think. Paying attention to your energy means you are response-able, and this gives you more capacity for impact and influence.

COACH IN YOUR POCKET POINTERS

⊙ *Stop! and breathe, take a moment, connect with yourself* before meetings, important phone calls, conversations and presentations. Creating this space, no matter how 'micro', will help you to act with more clarity and intention.

⊙ Notice your posture and your body language when you're under pressure or before heading into a meeting. Make a conscious shift, get unstuck and get centred.

⊙ Get moving! Get out from behind your desk. Stand up for your next call. Practise presentations while moving around. Take energising breaks.

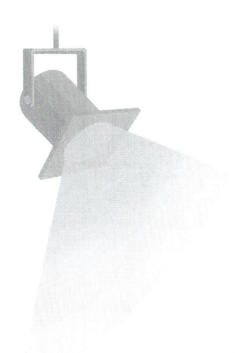

CHAPTER 2

Reawaken The Girl

As a child there was something you wanted to say, and you spend your whole life trying to say it.

(UNKNOWN)

I once heard a story about a little girl called Molly. One day, all the children in her class were drawing pictures. When the lunch bell rang, the teacher asked the children to stop drawing and put away their crayons. Molly took no notice of the teacher's instructions and kept on drawing.

'What are you drawing, Molly?' asked the teacher.

'I'm drawing a picture of God,' said Molly.

'No one knows what God looks like!' said the teacher.

Without looking up, Molly said, 'They will when I'm finished with my drawing.'

I love this story. I can see this little girl, completely immersed in her drawing, her cheeky determination to finish it, unfazed by lunch! Children are empowered with an innocence that grants them permission to believe in their own powers of creative expression and to believe that they can be anyone or do anything.

The little girl in you who could be anyone or do anything is within you still, so bring her along and keep her close!

Remembering

If you have access to a childhood photo album, have a look through it and reacquaint yourself with your girlhood. If you don't have an actual photo album, just sit or lie down, close your eyes and visualise the snapshots.

What did you love to do as a child? When were you completely immersed and 'carried away'? Who did you get to be? Who was your superhero? What did you love to play?

I remember devouring Nancy Drew novels and enacting the adventures of the intrepid girl detective through the house. I also worshipped a Mouseketeer called Annette Funicello – I would race home after school every day to watch the *Mickey Mouse Club* on television and learn her every song and dance. To this day I consider myself to be highly analytical and observant (the girl detective lives on), and for me, singing and dancing are life joys!

Enjoy your reflections and memories and notice any emotions and physical sensations that arise. The act of reawakening can be a bit noisy and demanding when you're listening!

REMEMBER THE GIRL EXERCISE

Here's a deeper exercise to reconnect with your inner girl:

- Choose a photo from that same album or dig one out from elsewhere. Enjoy rooting around in your archives for this little bit of archaeology.

- Once you've chosen a photo of yourself as a girl, place it where you can see it and set a timer for three minutes.

- Write without stopping. Begin each line with the words 'I remember...'

- Write fast and with a pen, not on a keyboard. This engages more of your physicality and emotions. Keep your pen moving. No editing.

- When the time's up, look over your list and *read it aloud*. Giving voice to these memories arouses your powerful storyteller.

- When you reflect on you as a girl, think about what is still true about you today. Jot these qualities or attributes down.

- Frame your girl photo and put her on your desk or make her your screen saver. Give the photo a caption.

- Keep your girl photo in view at all times.

If you're alive, you're creative

Creativity is unique in how it shows up in each and every one of us. All too often, the belief that creativity dwells only in the world of the arts and artists hijacks us. Hearing the words 'I'm not creative' spring from the voices of women – engineers, accountants, business-development directors, fund managers, academics, healthcare specialists – is painful, and it's such a myth.

News flash: if you're alive, you're creative!

In the everyday performance of our jobs and responsibilities, we forget parts of ourselves for periods of time, sometimes for whole chapters of our lives. Often, these parts are what we might call our creative selves, and they go dormant. The piano not touched for a decade, the favourite poems not read since school, the voice that once sang now speaking only workplace jargon behind a PowerPoint deck, the sketchbook abandoned for spreadsheets. Where is my doodler-dreamer, my secret songwriter, my fashion illustrator? So long lost.

Recognising this can be painful. How did this happen? It happened because our work-life persona said: 'No time for self-indulgence (a few minutes of daydreaming, a moment's meditation, a breath of inspiration). There's a job to get done here! Deliverables! Accountability! Performance!' We tell ourselves: 'At some point there will be time for me, but not right now.'

When we connect with our creativity, we are happier and healthier, more productive and purposeful, and more whole. While engaged in a creative act, we enter a state of flow, that mental state of immersion and energised focus named by pioneering psychologist, Mihaly Csíkszentmihályi.

Take a moment to write down the things you love doing, that make you feel in flow, energised, passionate, fascinated, immersed. Reflect on what these activities bring out in you and how they connect to your best self on the job. Your *acknowledgement of your creativity* can boost your professional story.

Stoke the fire

Please don't throw any of yourself away. Please listen to the stirring of something that has been dormant and is now reawakening in you. It is a moment of remembering yourself, a homecoming. Stoke that fire and unleash your unique creativity. It is a profoundly powerful resource for being at your best – as a professional player and as a human being.

Jane, a financial director, was firmly attached to her story that 'numbers are dull'. Given that her entire job was about numbers one way or another, it was a debilitating story. Or, to quote Hamlet, it was 'stale, flat, and unprofitable'.[8] One day Jane told me a bit of her life story and out flew her childhood passion for poetry and how images came to life for her in the language of poetry. So we turned our attention to poems, of course!

The more Jane started reading poems aloud, the more she gave herself permission to enjoy poetry again. It became a pleasurable way to connect with herself; *a warming up to herself.* Jane's big 'aha' moment came when she recognised that her poetry-reading voice was very different from her financial-presentations voice.

When Jane presented, she was credible and efficient but dull! Her presentations were blocks of dense information that she 'got through'. When she read poetry, Jane was thoughtful, nuanced and beautifully animated. Her love of language came through in her expression. How powerful it would be, she realised, if she approached her number-crunching presentations with more of her poetic self – if she made sense of the story behind the numbers for her listeners, made the story of those numbers compelling and valuable by investing her voice.

Happily for her boardroom audience, Jane quickly shed her rather buttoned-up 'safe pair of hands' (her words) approach and developed into a more confident and colourful presenter. Connecting with her long-dormant passion for poetry brought another dimension of her into the room. She inspired herself and she inspired others in the process.

So whether you lightly touch upon it (lift up that piano cover and tinker), reunite with it with a vengeance (turn your garden shed into a painting studio), explore new forms of it (join a choir, start a book club, visit art galleries) or just redefine what it is for you (cooking, putting together extraordinary travel itineraries): embrace your creativity. What it brings out in you is urgently needed on the job!

Play!

Years ago, at a brainstorming team meeting in Calgary, my colleagues and I sat around a large table covered with paints, pens and coloured paper. Our facilitator began the meeting by asking, 'Who here is an artist?' No one raised a hand. Self-conscious titters rippled through the room. After a pause, the facilitator said, 'OK. You're seven years old. Who's an artist?' Every hand shot up in the air, and we all laughed in recognition of the 'belief jump-start' she'd just given us.

Connecting with our inner child (we're seven, we rock!) gave us instant belief in our creativity. For the rest of the brainstorming meeting, we were artists at play. We used painting and collage to conjure up and capture ideas. We removed censors and judgement. We enjoyed fearless, raw, messy self-expression.

Not only was it liberating, it was productive! We came up with new ideas. We surfaced powerful insights. 'Playing at being seven' allowed us to break out of our habitual head zone ('I can't draw') and our default adult mindsets: the 'realistic', the 'practical' or the 'analytical' (take your pick, or all three). By entering the child zone of play, we tapped into the wellspring of our intuition and imagination.

The psychoanalyst Carl Jung believed that innovation, creating something new, was achieved more through play than through the intellect. Playing before analysing primes the pump for better-quality thinking. When we play, we open our bodies, hearts, minds, and senses. We are energised and in 'flow' – feeling spontaneous, full involvement and enjoyment in the process of the activity while in the act.[9]

Many women tell me, 'I haven't played since I was eight!' Clearly, it's time to return to that state of wonder. I'm sure you'll agree that children at play, in their immersion and flow, in their innocent confidence, are profound and magnificent role models. We need to stay in touch with that child within us!

Some of those wild and whacky 'ice breakers' you've experienced in training programmes are about getting into a state of play and breaking through the resistance of professional masks and job titles. When everyone takes the plunge, the room becomes an imaginary playground and invites laughter, abandon and connection. Playing is a fast track to bringing forth our humanity. In the act of playing together, we *warm ourselves up to ourselves, to one another and we warm up the environment itself in which we can make something meaningful happen.*

We may be surprised by the emotional impact we experience in moments of playing. This is because in the act of playing, all performances are perfect. We experience *complete acceptance.*

Playing isn't just for icebreakers in off-sites. Creatively exploring ideas and enacting, moving, and engaging with ideas by using all our senses and faculties – not just our heads – is *key for developing high performance.* Denise, a senior executive with a global recruitment firm, shared these thoughts about her experience of playing and enacting exercises in a leadership programme: 'Playing helped us all to override the analysis think-switch that we use pretty much exclusively, and just dive in… so exhilarating!'

Your own cast of characters

Emily, a CFO in the home entertainment industry, described her role in the business: 'I'm the one who keeps a tight grip on the money and says no.' She was aware that she was seen by others as 'locked down'.

In living her description of her role she was strait-jacketing her body, strangling her voice and restricting her choices for impact and engagement with her board. She habitually embodied the *tight grip* and the *no,* and she desperately wanted to find other options for her body language, behaviour and the story she was telling herself.

While working on a presentation during a coaching session, Emily and I did lots of playing. Sceptical at first, Emily ended up ad-libbing her way through her content as a playful experiment going completely off script. Not only did Emily show a daring, fun side of herself, she was a supercharged creative! Emily discovered she was at her best when she was improvising. Through improvisation, she brought her subject to life in a way that burst through her notes and slide deck.

Emily loved playing within the safety of the 'rehearsal room', and she took some of that creative courage with her back to work, where she dared to release more dynamic body language, more range in her voice and to make incrementally creative changes in the way she delivered her presentations and engaged with her team. Small changes can make a big impact. Emily brought more of herself through the door, the sky didn't fall in, and she got some great feedback, as her colleagues felt the benefit of better-quality engagement!

Sometimes the stories we tell about ourselves can become so entrenched that they lock down our identity ('I'm not creative'; I'm not the sort who…'; 'I wouldn't be authentic if I did that'). They shape our physicality and posture (crossed arms, legs twisted in a pretzel, collapsed chest, hunched shoulders, unconscious shifting and rocking when standing, etc). If this is true for you, it's time to step inside the rehearsal room with me. Let's hang a sign on the door that says 'Do Not Disturb: Serious Playing in Progress'.

PERSONAS EXERCISE

We're going to work *big* and work *physically* (did you expect anything else?).

- ⊕ Map out the story of you, from childhood to now. Start by taking a deep breath.

- ⊕ You could talk (you may want to record yourself). Describe yourself at different stages of your life through memories and key events.

- ⊕ You could draw a timeline on a large piece of paper or across a whiteboard and caption it according to each 'chapter' of your life.

- ⊕ You could plunder your archives and make a collage of photos of you through your life.

- ⊕ Move around so that your body participates in remembering the different versions of you.

- ⊕ When you finish, step back, pause, and take a deep breath. What a cast of characters, I'm sure you'll agree!

- ⊕ Now give each version of you a name. Create your avatars! Name the little girl rolling around with abandon, making snow angels, climbing trees (Wild Wendy); name the ingénue enjoying her beauty, being admired and awakening to her powers to seduce (Sexy Sadie); name the adventurer who backpacked around the world (Exploren Lauren); name the resilient and determined woman who worked nights or earned that degree she never thought possible (Ida the Invincible); name the action woman who ran a marathon or sailed a boat, the woman who fell in love, the woman who finds deep repose in playing the piano, and so on. Create as many as appear and as many as you want to acknowledge.

- Notice that making up fictitious, epic names helps you to recognise all the archetypes within you who have special voices and powers. To paraphrase Walt Whitman, you are vast and contain multitudes![10]

- Describe each character a little, and as you do, enact her physically. Any movement, gesture, posture or motif that conjures her up is great. Keep going to the next character and the next, describing her and physicalising her. Imagine you're in story-gym circuit training! You're doing great!

I hope this playing has been fun and purposeful for you. I hope it's given you the gift of reconnecting to your much greater range of voices and styles of behaviour than the one story has allowed you. Use that fabulous range of expressiveness and agility you have. Being authentic doesn't mean being one thing; it means having the capacity to tap into all your behaviour styles for your best performance. When you assert different energies, you are playing you: the Rottweiler, the Nurturer, the Motivator, the Challenger, the Seducer, the Authoritarian, the Creative and so on – all you. Play them as you need them!

COACH IN YOUR POCKET POINTERS

⊕ Make creativity dates with yourself: step inside that art gallery you pass every day, register for that workshop, join that choir, take out your sketchpad. Start today.

⊕ Reflect on the girlhood passions that still show up in you today. Keep your favourite photo of you as a girl visible at all times!

⊕ Give your different personas, traits and energy qualities an airing! Exercise them as required.

⊕ Remember: being authentically you does not mean being the same all the time. You possess a whole palette of expressive possibilities!

CHAPTER 3

Lead From Your Story

What's your story? It's all in the telling. Stories are compasses and architecture; we navigate by them.[11]

(REBECCA SOLNIT)

Your life story is your best asset

When working with teams, I most frequently hear this comment after the personal storytelling session: 'I've learned more about my colleagues in this one hour than I learned in working with them for a year!' In the act of storytelling, we are seen and heard with complete attention. We own our moment. Our stories reveal the collective humanity behind the job titles, and we begin stepping into our authentic presence.

There is only one of you in all time. You are unique and you are the author of your story, the person who can tell that story like no other. Your story is worthy of contemplation and needs expression. Within your life experiences – the ordinary, the epic, the dark and the light – there are important lessons, compelling insights and powerful messages to be revealed. You discover your beliefs and your commitment to them. Your stories live within you at a cellular level and shape your very physicality. Like the ground upon which you stand, your story is a place from where you can say, 'Yes, I know this.' *This is a place where I can trust what I know.*

Kafka's dramatic take on the subject is that 'a book must be the axe for the frozen sea inside us'.[12] I love the power of that image – a splitting open, an almost violent disruptor of the sleepwalker in us, the breaking through that which has become frozen (in time), shaking things up and releasing the stories once held captive in all the ice crystals.

Before your audience, team, clients and other stakeholders can care about what you know, *they have to know who you are*. That means *you* have to know who you are. This self-knowing comes from your life story. Hands down, it is your best asset.

What could be more powerful and effective in shaping your authentic voice and presence than your honouring and valuing the stories you carry within you? Wear them like a long, majestic cape that flows from you as you move through the world!

Your stories come in all shapes and sizes

Often our life stories begin with the stories of our ancestors – those who came before us and made it possible for us to arrive 'here'. These stories might be epic tales of journeys to new lands, of sacrifice and hardship to create a new life and learn new ways. Sometimes these stories are about continuity, roots, and tradition; about beliefs and community.

Most of us have character stories within our families: anecdotes or repeated tales about the antics and habits of a parent, grandparent, eccentric auntie or ever-reliable uncle. These ancestral stories – celebrated or quietly gathered across the day-to-day – are rich starting points for understanding the story of yourself. And, of course, your childhood stories have a profound influence on your future choices, paths and passions.

ANCESTRAL CONNECTION EXERCISE

◉ Sit comfortably, close your eyes and take a few deep breaths.

◉ Imagine all those ancestors who came before you, making it possible for you to be where you are today – those you knew and those you never knew.

◉ Conjure up the extraordinary trail of beings behind you, whose lives created the bridge to your own life here and now.

◉ Slowly come back to *now*.

When I was five years old, living in an apartment building in New York, a teenage girl who lived in the same building took me up the lift to the rooftop. When we stepped onto the roof, we saw a group of construction workers toiling away in the glaring sun. Many of them had T-shirts wrapped around their heads like turbans for protection.

That rooftop offered a panoramic view of the city. In my childhood innocence, having never seen this view nor turban-headed, shirtless men, I truly believed that I had magically stepped into another world.

The experience didn't last long, as my frantic mother found me and snatched me back inside, ferociously rebuking my tour guide! Although the adventure was short-lived, its impact on me and the sense I made of it was immense. I had caught my first glimpse of a world way beyond my own, a world that was exotic, mysterious, extraordinary and huge.

I'm convinced that the indelible impression it made on me motivated my nomadic adult life. I travelled around the world and lived in many countries and cultures. I would call this a micro-size story because I can tell it in a minute. But again, its impact on me was epic. That single moment was a story that packed a mighty punch.

What's so marvellous about the stories we choose to remember is that they can come in all sizes – from the recollection of a single moment to an epic tale – and we get to be the author. We can embellish them, re-jig them and exaggerate them. We can make them film-noir black-and-white or we can explode them into Technicolor! Purist accuracy be damned!

Our stories contain essential truths and significance for us when we tell them from the heart and the gut. What matters is the impact they have on us and the sense we make of them. For all I know, those men on the roof were firemen or actors on a set. We don't need to tyrannise our stories with facts. We're not historians!

Your stories cultivate your presence

Your stories feed your personal and professional life. By taking ownership of your stories, you tap into the powerful wellspring of your unique life force, clarify your strengths and ignite your courage.

Think of an anecdote about a remarkable person and their impact on you. Remember a time when you felt excluded. Conjure up the enchantment of a landscape you love. Capture the inventory of what makes you feel ferocious and want to rant! Think of a time you truly seized the day. Recall a time when you turned lemons into lemonade and salvaged the situation. Think of the funniest things that ever happened to you. From your metaphorical rocking chair, share significant lessons you've learned with a younger person or a childhood you. Mine your life experiences for stories.

There are great themes to be captured from your mining: achievement stories, failure stories, courage stories, inspiration stories, decision-making stories, stories about when you said yes to something and when you said no to something, turning-point stories, memorable-event stories, stories about seeing the world in a new way – epiphany stories, stories of adversity – crucible stories and many others.

Continue the list of stories that are calling for your attention. Get out your hardhat, gloves, goggles, picks and dusters and enjoy the archaeological dig for stories in your very own repository.

STORY INSIGHTS EXERCISE

⊙ Make a list of the stories you easily recall, the ones that leap out at you.

⊙ Next to each one, write, 'What I learned from this was...', and then fill in the blank. Don't overthink it. Work from the gut and work fast. For instance, on my own list is a story about working as a dishwasher at a performing arts camp and learning the value of earning my own money.

⊙ When you're done, read your lessons aloud. Enjoy your discoveries as your voice rings out and you feel the energy that comes from the clarity of your insights. You are in the process of cultivating your authentic voice.

Your stories are in service to others

Many years ago, while in my teens and dancing with a ballet company, I landed the role of the Russian doll in the ballet *Coppélia*. What thrilled me about this role was that I didn't have to be *en pointe* but got to dance folksy, earthy steps in tall red leather boots. How I loved those boots and how thrilled I was to have got this part!

On opening night, I performed my dance and then took my leave of the stage. Adrenaline pumping, I tore off the boots. That's when the terrible stomach-on-floor, rabbit-in-the-headlights moment hit: I was supposed to take a curtain call right after my dance! The audience was applauding and I had shed my boots! There was no way I could get them on again quickly enough.

I grabbed my boots, rushed back on stage, took a curtsey-like bow and held my boots up high with a final flourish. It was a triumph for me in two ways. First, I had acted as if my unorthodox curtain call was intentional, and the audience seemed to accept it. Second, I had chosen not to forego my curtain call just because my costume was incomplete and not in compliance with the ballet's rulebook. I chose to go out there, claim my applause – the audience's gift to me – and celebrate my success.

My achievement in this story was not that I got through a performance, or even that I invented a curtain call in a moment of crisis. My achievement was in recognising that my performance was in service to my audience and receiving their applause was part of a contract of respect and valuing. The ballet company's director was less impressed with my 'achievement' and reprimanded me mightily in front of the whole corps de ballet afterwards. Nevertheless, if I could do it again, I wouldn't change a thing!

Tell me a story about something you achieved and are proud of. I'd really love to hear it! Please, *please*, don't say these fatal words: 'I don't like to big myself up.' *Your stories are not for you alone. They are in service to others.* By telling your stories in service to others, you inspire and motivate them. You share learning and powerful messages with them. You give them an opportunity to reflect on their own lives, to feel more and dare more. Blowing your horn with a proud achievement story makes music for others to hear. It is a gift of permission to value themselves and claim the contributions they, too, can make. In shining your own spotlight, you enable others to see you and see themselves more clearly. Please use this magic mantra:

My stories are in service to others.

It will transform your habitual self-deprecating 'humility' into generous, open-hearted, self-valuing manna. With this mindset, you will experience an exciting and powerful shift in your presence. There will be no backing off, no apology in sight. Here, you are at your most authentic. Here, you are the artistic director of stories that connect you to powerful truths and a deeper self-knowing.

Let's get started on some storytelling! You can focus on an achievement story or you can choose one you captured from your ideas earlier in this chapter. Remember, to move others, you need to be moved yourself, so pick one that genuinely excites, energises and inspires you. Is there one in particular that leaps out and attracts your attention like no other? Commit to it and test-drive it to determine its impact on you and others.

TEMPLATE:
FAST TRACK STORY ORGANISER

Distil your story into the following four bullet points:

1. **The title of my story is** _____

    _____

    (Wear your imaginative storyteller's hat. Your title doesn't have
    to be literal. Hook your audience's attention)

2. **This is a story about (One sentence)** _____

    _____

    (Think movie-poster blurb; eg 'This is a story about a
    catastrophic climbing expedition')

3. **Picture this** _____

    _____

    (An image that symbolises your story or key message, that one
    larger-than-life slide projected on the screen)

4. **The message is** _____

    _____

    (What do you want your audience to think about? Care about?
    Be inspired about?)

You can download a larger version of this template by
going to ***www.theatre4business.com*** and clicking on the
Performing As YOU resources link on the website.

Now take a deeper dive and craft the full story from your distilled bullets by ad-libbing. Total improvisation. Tell your story without a script. Record it if that feels helpful. Let your spoken story be as raw and messy as it needs to be. Just experience getting it 'out' and surprise yourself!

On reflection, did you notice:

- Connection – What was truthful and meaningful to you in your story?

- Energy – Where did you experience energy in your body when you were speaking?

- Feeling – What were the highlight moments in your story?

Once you've experimented with your raw story, enjoy shaping and editing it. You can write it down or record it or both. You now have one great story to start your archive or to add to it.

Your life story and your career story are connected

If you're preparing for a promotion or transitioning into a new job or role, this is a perfect time to take stock of your career story and tell that story in a compelling way for those who need to hear it. By career story I don't mean your CV – I mean the narrative that underpins your bigger résumé and that prioritises *story* over *data*.

Try this: On a whiteboard or on flip-chart paper (work big!), draw a timeline and divide it according to your professional chapters, positions, or experience. Here are some examples.

Valerie, a regional director of business growth in a multinational chemical company, talked through the challenges she had overcome in her life and connected her strengths from those experiences to her capabilities in her career story.

Beth, a bio engineer, talked about the origins of her career path. She explained that her sibling had a rare disease and that an engineer had designed a medical device that massively increased her sibling's life expectancy, which was inspirational to Beth. She developed her story to illustrate the ways in which her love of engineering played out and made an impact on her organisation.

Donna drew two parallel timelines – life events and career events – and captured the significant links between them. She used 'I can' moments from both her life and work; for example, making the key speech at a family milestone celebration, sailing a boat single-handed, delivering increased profits in her market sector, standing up and being counted in a critical moment on the job, and so forth. This produced a confidence and self-belief 'map' that helped Donna see clearly the value she brought to her organisation and how it played out. She was able to summarise her key leadership assets and how they would serve her in her next role.

Another approach was Meg's. She was leading a new team in a large tech firm. Meg began by storyboarding her career (chapters of jobs, roles, responsibilities). For each section, she summarised her key achievements and the strengths they illuminated; eg 'I am a great decision-maker, I exercise astute judgement, I enjoy relationship building one-to-one, I am energised by winning,' etc. Finally, Meg looked into her personal life story for evidence of these assets and how they operated in her life outside the office.

The big 'aha' moment for everyone was in seeing the connections between their career and life stories and feeling a powerful sense of integration. They were in the act of bringing both their 'outside' and 'inside' selves into play, of bringing more of themselves through the door.

Your tale of two personas

It's not always easy 'bringing more of ourselves through the door' at work. Companies have their cultures, their spoken and unspoken rules and codes ('That's the way we do things here'), their unique jargon, their dress codes, and, very often, their male role models, who define what professional looks and sounds like.

Let's hack our way through the low-hanging fruit to get to a clear space. See if you recognise any of these thoughts:

- 'My boss tells me I'm too emotional.'

- 'I don't take time for me because I should be earning my fees, not meditating.'

- 'I feel like I'm going to be found out, that I don't know what I'm doing.'

- 'I don't get in on the discussion at the right moment to make my points heard and then someone else makes the point.'

- 'Others often get the credit for my ideas and I let that happen.'

- 'I wish I could use more humour.'

- 'I'm lucky to have this office but I haven't looked out the window at the view for a long time.'

- 'I need more gravitas.'

- 'I get flustered if I don't know an answer in the Q&A.'

- 'The slide deck has to have twenty-five slides.'

- 'I'm struggling with the message I have to give.'

- 'I can't say no to requests so I get more and more work piled on me.'

- 'My boss expects me to respond to emails late at night and on weekends.'

Just reading this list makes me feel as if I'm walking through a petrified forest full of thorns and brambles. But in the clearing is a woman dancing in the moonlight, laughing at the gods, running with the wolves.

It's easy to see how, over time, the routine, company culture and habits we fall into create professional masks and heighten our conformity, risk aversion, and fear of failure or standing out for the wrong reasons. But companies are communities, and their conventions are entirely human-made, capable of becoming mythologised. Over time, those myths are perpetuated and become entrenched. They become the story.

In response to the tyrannical 'That's the way we do things here', one might ask, 'Who makes the rules?' Why not break the rules if they don't serve us? Storytelling can help us to see the big picture more clearly, make sense of our personal and professional selves and provide evidence of our growth and gifts. Our storytelling can make us more courageous by making us whole.

Getting to know you

Remember those habitual stories we discussed earlier, in Chapter 2, 'Your Own Cast of Characters', the ones that go unchallenged?

- 'I'm not the kind of person who…'

- 'I never perform well in these situations'

- 'That's just not me'

These know-it-all voices can take up an awful lot of airtime, and we let them! A particularly dramatic example of this is Ava's experience. Ava asked for coaching to 'find her voice'. She explained that her visibility was rising in the male-dominated automotive sector. She had been invited to give a series of keynote talks to large audiences and she wanted to sound more confident.

We were in a room that was well protected from outside noise and had good acoustics, but I struggled to hear Ava. Her voice sounded tight and whispery. When I asked her to speak up, she stopped, blushed and said: 'I can't. This is how I speak. And I'll always use a microphone.'

Ava believed that with a few tips and techniques she could get through her keynotes with the aid of a microphone. But no amount of microphone volume was going to make her talks compelling. Why? Because when I listened to Ava speaking, I had no idea who she was. Why would anyone listening to Ava's keynote be inspired, moved or persuaded by her ideas or trust her if they didn't know who she was and if she didn't share her humanity with them?

We threw away the script and the agenda. Ava told me her life story, a story of loss and hard work and reinvention. It took a few starts; her eyes welled up, and she got short of breath, anxious and stuck. I encouraged her to keep going *through* her tears. I asked her to move as she wished and as her emotions led her: to walk, to sit, to stand, to make eye contact, to face the wall; to *let her body lead*; to break all the rules. There *were* no rules.

In this rehearsal space, Ava bravely explored her story. She didn't stop. Not when the going got tough and she was close to tears. Not when she actually cried. Not when she moved and not when she was still. Her story found new life. Her story found new words. Her words started to pour forth with pace, with volume, with tones, with intensities. They carried weight. She was unstoppable. When she came to the end of her story, Ava looked and sounded very different.

Ava had broken through her fear of expressing her emotions.

By following role models who believed vulnerability was off-limits in the boardroom, she had left her full self at the door. There was nothing Ava needed to learn about vocal exercises or speaking techniques.

By facing the fear of an old story – 'If I start crying I won't stop' – and by honouring the wisdom and experience behind her tears, Ava found her voice. She may always prefer microphones, but now she can still be heard if the technology breaks down. Even if Ava chooses never to tell personal stories in her talks, she has experienced their power and can show up in her full humanity when she walks to the podium, takes a breath and begins. She will inspire her audiences with the weight of her presence and her words.

COACH IN YOUR POCKET POINTERS

- ⊕ Start creating your personal repository of stories, noting the lessons learned or insights discovered from these stories.

- ⊕ Share a personal story with a trusted colleague and a friend and get their feedback on the story's impact and message.

- ⊕ Storyboard or timeline your career, noting key achievements, strengths and drivers. Reflect on how these connect to your personal life.

- ⊕ Remember, your stories are in service to others. Value your story and be generous about sharing it.

- ⊕ Get to know the stories of those you lead.

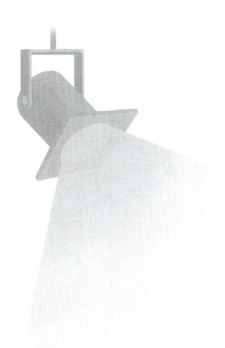

CHAPTER 4

The Now Of Presence

We convince by our presence.[13]

(WALT WHITMAN)

Presence is about being present

In the Queen's House on the magnificent grounds of the Royal Observatory Greenwich is an extraordinary portrait of Elizabeth I circa 1588. She's decked out in ruffles and pearl-encrusted splendour, a globe of the world at her hand, and looks formidable, invulnerable and idealised. Near her portrait is a description of the room where she received her courtiers, called the Queen's Presence Chamber. The portrait and the chamber were designed to lift the Queen to divine status, mask her 'frail womanhood' and imbue her with the highest aura of power. Her presence was an embodied symbol of mystery and the unknowable.

Cut to Academy Awards season: the papers are filled with images of stars on red carpets looking poised under a barrage of flashing cameras and adoring fans reaching out for autographs. Ever image conscious, these stars of the screen seem to have unerring instincts about how to show their most flattering angles, profiles and smiles. In those immortal words of Gloria Swanson, they're always 'ready for [their] close-up'.[14]

The kind of presence I'm talking about, though, isn't about masks of power or the red carpet and cameras. It's about being completely present in the moment. The actress Julianne Moore once said in an interview that 'your presence can bring out their presence, you elevate *everything*'.[15] I think she was talking about presence as the quality of engagement with others you create.

Your presence allows you to see and hear other people, and allows them to feel seen and heard. When you are fully present, creating real engagement, you are giving and attracting attention. When you leave the room, your presence lingers and inspires confidence and commitment in those around you because they have had a meaningful and positive experience.

Stand up straight

Many years ago, when I was living in Ireland and travelling throughout the country as an arts correspondent, I interviewed a woman who ran a ballet school on her dairy farm. She told me that her motivation for starting the school was down to one thing: poor posture.

Watching a national beauty pageant, she said she saw many girls parading around in bathing suits and high heels with drooping, self-conscious posture and decided there and then that Ireland's girls needed more pride. And so it came to pass that this intrepid pioneer gave ballet classes to slouching girls for miles around, helped them stand tall and turned many of them into ballerinas.[16]

I'm constantly surprised to see so many incredibly smart, talented women in the corporate workplace present poor posture: sitting hunched over in their chairs with crossed arms and legs, looking as if they're tied up in knots; or standing in a 'pretzel' with their feet criss-crossed, looking tentative at best or perilously off balance; or slumping over to one side in their chairs, looking practically comatose; or standing and rocking back and forth, looking as if they'd rather be anywhere but where they are.

If you recognise yourself in any of these descriptions, or any variation of them, listen up: When you sit up straight and stand up straight, you have instant gravitas. You are mighty. End of story.

POSTURE EXERCISE

Try these three postures (exaggerate them as much as you can):

⊕ **Posture 1** – Sit down in a slump, shoulders and head drooping, face glum, as if you're despondent. You can also try a walking version of this. Walk slowly, head drooping, eyes cast down, as if feeling the weight of the world on your shoulders.

⊕ **Posture 2** – Sit with your hands behind your head and put your feet up on your desk. Look up and out as if daydreaming

or envisioning something 'out there' that
feels full of wonder or hope or beauty.
Try a version of this standing up tall with
your feet apart and hands on your hips.
Gaze outwards to an imaginary horizon,
or as if you're proudly surveying your land
like a pioneer woman in the Wild West.

⊕ **Posture 3 –** Sit up straight and lift your
arms high, palms facing up. Raise your
face to the ceiling or sky and smile as big
as you can, as if you're in one of those ads
for toothpaste that gives you gleaming
teeth and a sparkling smile. Now try this
standing up. Really fling your whole being
upwards, arms and face to the sky, as if
you're a mighty goddess laughing at the
universe.

⊕ Notice the energy you experience from
posture to posture. Notice the mood or
attitude shifts you experience as you
change from one state to another.

⊕ Now try out the three postures again
and speak aloud – anything at all. Notice
the different tone, volume and quality of
your voice from one posture to the next.
Notice how your body and your voice are
connected!

Your name is your reputation

The comedian Michael McIntyre performs a piece about meeting someone at a cocktail party and not hearing their name the first time they introduce themselves. In the skit, he asks them to repeat it, and of course, he doesn't hear their name the second time either. By this point he's too mortified to ask again, so he feigns comprehension: 'Nice to meet you, *murphmmmm*.'[17]

Why do we perpetuate this lazy, stingy habit? Why do we mumble our names or rush past them as if to get it over with as quickly as possible?

Your name is the first utterance of your identity, as powerful as the first words in a play or movie, the first sentence in a novel, the first note in a symphony, the first mark on a canvas, and the first gesture in a dance – a beginning that leads to a bigger story.

At the Banff Centre, in the Canadian Rockies, I learned the ritual of creating an Inuksuk, originally performed by the Inuit. Everyone makes a large circle and one by one, participants place a stone on the ground in the centre, creating a natural installation. Originally, the Inuit performed this ritual to say 'people have been here'. The Inuksuk acted as a guide to others in a landscape with no discernible landmarks. In the placing of our symbolic stones, we were committing to a moment in time, a moment of pure presence, offering a piece of collective legacy. In essence, each person's name was on the stone they placed.

Your name is the gateway to your life story, and that story is the DNA of your unique, authentic presence. Your name matters, so get interested in its sound and let's hear it the first time around!

Pause for presence

I love art galleries. Besides the sheer aesthetic pleasure of looking at paintings and the world of colour, texture, scale and subject matter, I love the big airy spaces of galleries, and I particularly love the way pictures are framed. In fact, I often fall for the frames more than the pictures!

There's a reason why pictures are framed. Frames create a unique platform for our attention, a distinctive space in which we are invited to dwell awhile and engage our senses – a space to process our experience.

Think of a pause when you're speaking like a frame around a picture. When you pause, you frame your words. Pausing gives you a chance to breathe and gives your audience a chance to hear and process your words. Pausing, like framing, allows you the opportunity to highlight moments and emphasise key words and points. You are giving your audience the gift of understanding and maximising their engagement.

More critically, pausing bestows on the speaker physical presence and presence of mind.

'When we feel powerful, we speak more slowly and take more time,' says Amy Cuddy. 'We don't rush. We're not afraid to pause. We feel entitled to the time we're using.'[18]

For my money, it's the other way around. When we speak more slowly, take more time, don't rush, and take pauses, we feel much more powerful – because we're more grounded. We are literally standing our ground. From here, we step into our fullest presence.

Your presence embodies your stories

Your life stories are the DNA of your signature style, voice and presence. Sharing your stories is one of the most powerful things you can do for yourself. Entrepreneur Nely Galán says, 'In your pain is your brand.'[19] She's referring to the stories we would rather forget, the stingers that are almost too much to look at, the ones that touch on our vulnerability, but that can give us the greatest insights and wisdom to share with others.

When I was in the fifth grade, I was assigned a project about architecture. My dad and I worked for weeks building a windmill out of sugar cubes. Then we mounted it on a platform, ready for proud presentation at the school exhibition. I was so excited on the day I took my windmill to school – I couldn't wait for everyone to see it. The route down the corridor was packed with rowdy kids. A boy crashed into me and over I tumbled. *Splat!* went the windmill, a catastrophe of sugar dust. I was distraught.

But worse than that was landing heels over head with my skirt up and all the kids taunting that they could see my underwear. My humiliation was seismic. A kind teacher helped me up and dusted me down. He gave me a broom and got me sweeping. All the while he reassured me that he'd seen my windmill before its destruction and thought it was a brilliant success. I remember focusing on the sweeping and on his words.

Although I didn't know it then, I was rehearsing a 'stand up straight and realise who you are, that you tower over your circumstances' moment (thanks, Maya Angelou).[20] Our crucible stories often bring out our strengths and allow us to bear witness to ourselves. We've got skin in the game. It has cost us something. And when we invest in these stories, we ultimately reap the reward of deeper self-knowing and stand in our full grace and integrity.

'Act as if' and whistle a happy tune

It would be a colossal understatement to say I'm a fan of musicals. I'm crazy about them. I know they aren't everyone's cup of tea (some of my best friends avoid them at all costs!). But I can't understand what's not to like about singing and dancing your way through love, betrayal, perils, triumphs, dastardly deeds and happy endings. And beyond the song-and-dance spectacle, there's a world of wisdom in the lyrics.

One such inspiring song is 'I Whistle a Happy Tune', from *The King and I*, written by Rodgers & Hammerstein. I first saw it on Broadway as a star-struck adolescent. Gertrude Lawrence played the English governess (and singer of the song) and Yul Brynner played the king. I was so enraptured watching them waltzing around the Court of Siam I don't think I exhaled for the duration of the entire scene.

The governess sings the song to her young son just as they arrive in Siam, where she will be serving the king as governess to the many children of his court. Every verse of the song is about tricking oneself into a state of fearlessness, confidence and gravitas by striking brave poses and thinking big inside. In the act of singing the song to her son, the governess becomes more and more positive herself; if ever there was a perfect display of 'getting into a positive state', this is it.

If you don't know the song, please take a moment right now and look it up. Print the lyrics. If you do know the song, stand up and sing it now! See what I mean?

'I Whistle a Happy Tune' is the best 'acting as if' tool I know.

'Acting as if' boils down to one word: intention. When you set a clear intention (to act as if you're fearless, in this case), your body, your voice, your energy and your beliefs follow through most elegantly. When you set a clear intention, you can shift from tentative to confident, or any quality you desire. Your mind is the director of You Inc. All it's waiting for is its mission from you.

So set your intention and 'act as if'. Start with 'I Whistle a Happy Tune' and see how quickly you can upgrade your mojo. In the words of William James, *'I don't sing because I'm happy; I'm happy because I sing!'* Oh, and please go see a musical!

Just say 'thank you'

At a panel discussion hosted by a prominent global science organisation, I was struck by the unique and vibrant appearance of one of the panellists. She had an audacious, distinctive haircut and an attention-grabbing dress sense that appealed to me enormously.

At the coffee break, I sought her out. 'Great haircut and outfit,' I told her. 'You look fabulous.'

With a delighted smile, she looked me in the eyes and said, 'Thank you!' As I started to walk away, she added, 'I've been practising saying "Thank you" and not deflecting compliments.'

I loved her honesty, and that she'd let me in on her secret piece of personal development.

In her 'thank you' stance, this lively, esteemed young scientist accepted the gift of my compliment with lightness and ease. She was in balance, in flow and owning the authentic expression of herself.

How refreshing it is to be on the terra firma of simple, dignified etiquette rather than getting bogged down in the muck of deflection, denial and self-deprecation. Why is it so hard to utter 'thank you'? Accepting a compliment is an act of presence and the very opposite of arrogant. It is the gracious act of receiving a gift.

Think about the last time someone gave you a gift. Visualise it in its beautiful wrapping. Now imagine that instead of holding the gift with an expression of gratitude and delight, you dodge out of the way and let it drop to the floor! Shocking and insulting, wouldn't you agree?

Deflecting compliments or praise is the clumsy and tedious equivalent of dropping a gift on the floor. Reframing a compliment as an act of receiving a gift will keep you in the positive mindset of appreciating the gift giver as you reach forward to receive it.

The more you practise, the more fluent you'll become in the act of *appreciative receiving*. This is gravitas and presence at its most graceful. The next time someone gives you the gift of a compliment or praise, make their day and just say 'thank you'. Not another word is needed.

COACH IN YOUR POCKET POINTERS

⊙ Standing or sitting, hold out your right arm, palm up, and say your first name (as if your name is an object on the palm of your hand). Now hold out your left arm, palm up, and say your last name. Notice how this opens your body and allows you to articulate your name clearly.

⊙ Mime taking off a pullover. Really exaggerate this gesture – make it as big as you can. Feel your posture instantly lift as you pull the jumper over your head.

⊙ Don't rush it! Pause for breathing space, clarity and effect when speaking.

⊙ Set a clear intention and 'act as if.'

⊙ When you receive a compliment, praise or positive feedback, say 'thank you' and imagine being handed a beautifully wrapped gift.

CHAPTER 5

Your Impact And Influence Is Not One-Size-Fits-All

I know who I was when I got up this morning, but I think I must have been changed several times since then.[21]

(LEWIS CARROLL)

In the course of a month, a week or even one day you probably engage with an astonishing number of environments – from making presentations to leading team meetings, giving feedback to a direct report, hosting global conference calls and much more.

Being alert to your environments, to the different spaces you occupy, to the people in the room, is vital to working and living effectively. Understanding the impact that environments have on you and the impact you can have on your environments is critical for getting the results you want.

Let's start with the obvious: your immediate work environment. Take a good look around, as if for the first time, at this place in which you spend so much of your time – your base camp. Is it a private office? A shared office? A cubicle in an open-plan? Do you work from an office at home? What do you like about it? What don't you like about it? How does it support you? What are the challenges in this space?

Patsy, a team leader for regional sales in her business unit, told me that she loves her ergonomic chair and curvaceous desk but that she feels anxious every time she has a customer call, knowing she can be heard by her colleagues in their shared office.

Margot, who works in publishing, loves the buzz of her open-plan office and the feeling of being part of a vital mission, connected to others. However, Margot admits to being easily distracted and pulled into the peripheral conversations around her, which can drain her energy.

Environments impact your performance

Environments have a big impact on how we think, feel and behave. In the field of education, there's a mass of evidence on the relationship between environments and learning. In the field of neuroscience, much research has been published on human adaptation to environments and the influence of environments on shaping behaviours.

A few years ago, I held a workshop at a European pharmaceuticals HQ. Everything was state of the art. The problem was the air. The central air-conditioning system had shut down and the windows in the room couldn't be opened. This had a huge impact on everyone's energy, as you can imagine!

By the early afternoon our group was dragging. There were complaints of headaches. One woman felt sick. One woman fainted. It was clear that our environment wasn't going to serve our learning.

We decamped into the corridors, the cafeteria, the lounge areas and an outdoor terrace. Shifting environments, we went from being zombies to being rebels to being creative, agile learners. It was clear we couldn't adapt to the status quo; rather, we had to create the conditions we needed to meet our objectives – to have a transformative learning experience.

I'm certainly not advocating abandoning your office as a first step in your environmental awareness! What I am advocating is observing and reflecting on what your environment is like. Paint a picture of it for yourself and take a moment to capture how you *are in it*.

What small, safe intervention(s) could you perform in your environment that would make a difference to how you felt, behaved, performed? Do you need to find a way to signal 'genius at work – do not disturb' time to your distracting colleagues? Do you need to stand up and look out the window while making those customer calls? In other words, how can you take some ownership of your environment to serve yourself better?

I'll never forget a keynote by a leader in the oil industry. She came into the auditorium amid applause and immediately walked over to the table covered in water bottles left from the previous panellists. Then she calmly cleared away every bottle, creating a good-humoured assembly line with the bemused stagehands. When she'd decluttered the space to her satisfaction, she walked to the microphone and said, 'I'm here to talk about oil, not water.' There was thunderous applause and laughter from the audience. It was a memorable moment of witnessing someone *taking ownership of her environment* and creating the conditions that would enable her, and therefore her audience, to focus on the subject.

What will your decluttering look like? What's one small action you can take to create the conditions you need to improve your performance?

Adele often had meetings in a rather sterile room with fluorescent lighting on the thirtieth floor of an office tower. During a coaching session to help Adele prepare for a big sales pitch, she seemed stuck. The environment wasn't supporting her or unlocking any creativity. I asked her to stand at the window and ad-lib her pitch using anything she saw as a metaphor or connection to her subject.

'I haven't looked out of the window for a very long time!' Adele admitted. As she did so, she saw a huge crane and a panoramic picture of building activity. Suddenly, a stream of ideas and fresh language about building and growth flowed out of Adele with astonishing fluency and enlivened her pitch content dramatically. By taking a moment to look out of the window and see her environment with fresh eyes, Adele pressed her refresh button and got herself unblocked.

Understand the story of your environments

In Chapter 1, you connected to your body as your first environment. You took a moment to *Stop! and breathe*, and to find a moment of stillness before rushing into action. Hopefully you've started doing this regularly, but if you haven't you can start now!

Next, you stepped back to take a good look at your most familiar work environment and determine what it's like and how it affects you, positively and negatively. Perhaps you discovered that there's one small action you can take immediately to shift it so that it supports you rather than draining or challenging you.

Now, let's consider all the environments in which you operate at work and make a map of them. An environment map is a visual story. Work big for this exercise. I know I'm repeating myself. I want to keep reminding you that when you work big, you involve the whole of your mind and body. Doing so, you use more brain power and unlock your capacity to see clearly and engage fully.

ENVIRONMENT MAP EXERCISE

⊕ Using a blackboard, a whiteboard, flip-chart paper or any other surface that allows you to *work big*, draw a map of all the environments (places, spaces, people) you engage with in the course of a typical workday (or week or month).

⊕ 'I can't draw!' I hear you say. OK, so pretend you're seven years old. Remember Molly? This doesn't require any artistry or fine draughtsmanship. Circles, lines, arrows, rectangles, squiggles, crosses and stick figures will do – just symbolise all those environments you operate in. Spare no detail! This is a 'lived reality' board! Be as inclusive as you can.

⊕ Here are some examples: Do you have weekly team meetings in a particular room, on a particular day with a specific number of people? Draw the table, indicate the number of people around it with crosses and so on. Do you chair the meetings? If so, make your cross large. Do you host global conference calls dealing with different time zones? Where do these happen? How many people are involved? Do you conduct 1:1s in your office? Show that on your map. Do you have formal board meetings? When and where

do they happen? Do you give presentations?
Where do they happen? How large is your
audience?

◉ Illustrate *all* your working environments on
the paper. Your map should be populated
with as many examples as possible. If most
of your environments are meetings, it's vital
to map out the differences between those
meetings: Do they all involve the same people,
at the same time and in the same place?
Are they different meetings with different
stakeholders? Do not generalise. Be specific.

Your environment map reveals surprising data

When you're done creating your environment map,
step back and admire your handiwork! Surprised?
It's amazing to discover just how many environments
you 'perform' in, isn't it? You sure pack a lot in!
Now return to your map and tag each environment
with two bullet points:

- The purpose (What is this meeting, call,
  presentation for?)

- The result (What do I want to happen as a
  result of this scenario?)

Once you've created your tags on your environment map, step back again and ask yourself this question: *How do I prepare for each of these environments?* You might say:

- 'I always prepare the agenda for my team meetings in advance.'

- 'I've thought about the feedback I'm going to give to my colleague.'

- 'I've pulled together a great slide deck for the presentation.'

- 'I've got handouts and a list of anticipated questions.'

Of course you do and have all these things. You're a professional! So let me pose the question differently: How do you prepare *yourself* for these environments and scenarios? How do you need to show up?

Are the environments of team meetings, one-to-one feedback conversations, and PowerPoint presentations the same? No!

Do you play each of these roles – team-meeting leader, feedback initiator and presenter – the same way? No!

Do you want to be seen and heard the same way in each environment and in each role you play? No!

Do you see where I'm going with this?

Be an environmental activist

Content preparation aside, let's focus on how you prepare yourself to be at your authentic best and have the impact and influence you want in the different environments you operate in. You've clarified the purpose of your environments and what you want to happen as a result of your engagement in the scenarios.

Now it's time to do an impact and influence audit. Looking at your environments and scenarios and their objectives, reflect on how you show up in each one.

- Think about your energy levels and how some might require more *oomph* than others.

- Think about your body language and whether you need to change it up for the impact you need to make or the rapport you need to create or the deep listening you need to show.

- Notice if your intention and your presence are aligned for what needs to happen.

If you're noticing that you think a lot about content preparation but very little about self-preparation, you're not alone.

If you think that performing differently in different environments means you're not being authentic, you're not alone.

These are the two most common stories lived out in the business world. They are nothing more than default stories, the 'managing OK' and 'comfort zone' way of doing things. As you've seen in Chapter 2, from the litmus test 'Your Environment Map Reveals Surprising Data', different environments ask different things of you to create maximum engagement and buy-in. Your impact and influence is not one-size-fits-all.

Going forward, to prepare yourself, *Stop! and breathe* and ask: 'What is needed here?' How do I need to show up? Clarify your intention and purpose. Calibrate your energy and investment accordingly. Notice the results!

Your magical energy wardrobe

Mark Zuckerberg, of Facebook fame and fortune, said in an interview that he wears the same thing every day – a grey T-shirt and jeans – because it cuts down on his decision-making time. His fashion default became his brand as well as his modus operandi.[22]

However well this 'uniform habit' serves Zuckerberg in his time management, it doesn't serve you well in your performance management. Why? Because performance is about managing your energy, and each performance requires different energy. You don't need a uniform. You need a wardrobe.

Your default zone may be a comfortable, efficient place in which to operate, but it can all too easily become your one-size-fits-all uniform, that grey T-shirt. Imagine going to the cinema or theatre and seeing the actors wearing a grey T-shirt no matter what character they were playing or what story they were telling!

A more resourceful and effective way to prepare yourself to be your best is to ditch the grey T-shirt and 'dress for the part', energetically speaking. This means getting into the right state of body and mind for the role you're performing, what you want to achieve and how you want to influence your audience.

Think of all those different scenarios you surfaced in your environment map: important one-to-one conversations, team meetings, pitches and presentations, video conference calls, and everything in between. Take a moment to visualise yourself in those situations. Do they require different types of engagement and performance from you? You bet they do!

We all have our default styles, our 'uniforms'. Maxine, in banking, habitually spoke in a soft, monotone voice. She presented a relaxed demeanour that signalled her preference for one-to-one conversations. Her body language was reflective and inward-focused. So far so good. But how do you think that worked out for Maxine in all her scenarios? She got some pretty tough feedback in her performance review about needing to 'come forward more', 'speak up' and 'sound more interested in what she was talking about' when engaging with larger audiences.

To show up effectively in the different roles you play, in the different environments you play in, you need to calibrate your energy. The energy, tone, pace, body language, presence and engagement required for one-to-ones is different from that required for formal boardroom meetings, and different again from that required for virtual conference calls, for presentations and pitches, and for team meetings.

I'll say it again. One size does not fit all! You need to tune up the way you turn up!

Your three key pieces

It's time to *step into your energy wardrobe and 'dress the part'*. What's great about this wardrobe is that it's lean and portable – strictly hand luggage. There are only three pieces in it.

If you're a numbers person, think of your energy wardrobe in terms of intensities:

- 1 (relaxed, natural)

- 5 (leaning in, eyeball to eyeball)

- 10 (stand and deliver)

If you prefer words, think of your energy wardrobe in these terms:

- Casual

- Intense

- Panoramic

If you're more kinaesthetic, think of your energy wardrobe as having 'states':

- Conversation

- Campfire

- Auditorium

We are not one-dimensional, and neither are the environments we perform in. Making a conscious choice about how to calibrate our energy for the role we're playing – how to 'dress for the part' – requires answering one question:

How can I best serve my audience in this moment?

The great news is you can mix and match your energy wardrobe to fit any scenario. For example, you can do 'campfire' energy while sitting around a table. Lean in, make eye contact, take your time, gather attention and put your point on the table for all to look at. You can also do 'auditorium' energy while sitting around a meeting table by sitting up straight, putting your hands on the table and creating a bigger space and 'force field' around you, being more 'vertical', thinking 'stand' even while sitting.

Observe how you shift gears, how different you feel and sound in each of these states of energy. Notice how each of these states helps support your intention. Enjoy mixing up your energy wardrobe as needed!

In the course of a meeting or a presentation, you have many choices for impact. Sometimes:

- You'll need to sit back and see the bigger picture around the table or in the room

- You'll need to lean forward for laser-sharp focus

- You'll need to 'stand tall', whether in front of a room or sitting at a table

- You'll need to pause to gather attention and make your words land

- You'll need to put your audience of one at ease

- You'll need to motivate and energise a roomful of people

So start trying on and trying out your energy wardrobe and notice the results.

Once you get the hang of having an energy wardrobe and choices for impact, you'll be able to 'change clothes' with ease because you'll have clear intentions. You'll ask,

'What needs to happen here?' and your body language, voice, energy and quality of engagement will follow.

The secret sauce of impact and influence is the quality of engagement you create for others. How *you* are affects how *they* are.

ENERGY WARDROBE EXERCISE

Practise speaking aloud a brief key message you often have to deliver (a couple of sentences, max), or just a simple statement, in these three states of energy:

1. **Conversation**: Sit back in your chair, relaxed. This is 'hanging out' mode. Everything is nice and easy. You're comfortable in your own skin.

2. **Campfire**: Sit forward in your chair and rest your elbows on your knees, as if you're leaning towards the warmth of a fire. This is a mode of intensity, of storytelling, of pulling your audience in, of creating enchantment. You're slow, deliberate and inclusive. You make strong eye contact and connect with everyone around you. You pause for impact. You 'hold' the space.

3. **Auditorium**: This is your 'stand and deliver' mode. You have a big field of vision, an imaginary stage to move on, perhaps even

a podium. In this state, you're in your fullest and boldest presence, communicating inspirationally and projecting your voice and gaze outward and upward. Think 'spotlight' and 'standing ovation' to maximise your practice.

When you're surviving, not thriving

What scenario gets the better of you? In what scenario are you not at your best or most effective? It might be a situation you can't stand. Perhaps you've built up resentment about it. Perhaps it leaves you feeling frustrated or drained. Perhaps you try to avoid it altogether. Perhaps you had one bad experience and the story of it has stayed with you and become mythologised in an unhelpful way and is holding you up. Old stories can become a habit!

Think of an example of a challenging situation where you're not at your best. Be as detailed and forensic about this story as possible. If you have a friend or trusted colleague you can share this with, doing so will be super helpful.

NEGATIVE NARRATIVE EXERCISE

Tell the story as if you're in it right now – as if the 'movie' is playing. Spare no details of what it's like to be in the situation.

⊙   What does it look like?

⊙   What does it sound like?

⊙   Where are you?

⊙   What's the physical set-up?

⊙   Who's with you?

⊙   What's going on in your body and with your emotions?

Notice an attitude that comes over you. If you're doing this on your own, write down key thoughts, feelings and words that jump out.

If you could change the scenario (avoidance not an option!) to get the results you want, what could that look like? Might you prepare your mindset differently? Listen longer without interrupting? Be more relaxed and settled in your body to transmit more ease? Ask more questions? Exercise more empathy? Show more interest and energy? Name what you want to happen that's not already happening.

Enthral me with the details of your effectiveness

Well done for stepping into your challenge story and staying with it through the discomfort! Now, have a fresh look at your environment map and note where you're at your best. Again, if you can share your story with a friend or colleague, great! If you're doing this solo, consider your 'at your best' story in as much detail as possible.

POSITIVE NARRATIVE EXERCISE

Run the movie and relive the experience of your 'at your best' story as fully as possible in the present tense.

⊕   What is it like?

⊕   Where are you?

⊕   Who are you with?

⊕   What are you doing?

⊕   What do you look like? Sound like? Feel like?

Totally blow your horn! Spare no details!
Claim the I big time! Begin each sentence with the words 'When I'm at my best I am...'

Enjoy making your inventory of 'strength assets'. Write these assets down.

If you're working with a friend or colleague, ask for their feedback after they hear your story: 'Having heard your story, these are qualities and strengths that I "got" about you.' Thank them for their feedback and write it down.

Put your resources to work

OK. You've described what it's like to be in your 'at your best' state and you've gathered your inventory of greatness. It might include things such as 'When I'm at my best I am a great listener, passionate, energetic and enthusiastic, decisive, a creative problem solver, good at putting people at ease and asking the killer questions', and so on. Let's return to your challenging environment, where you are not at your best, and apply one or some of those 'at your best' strengths. Put those assets to work!

- What behaviour or strength do you have in abundance when you're at your best that you could apply to your challenging scenario?

- What is one thing you could do differently? Say differently? Think about differently?

- What is one thing you could let go of?

- What is one way you could prepare yourself differently before going into that scenario?

- What could happen as a result?

Try it out at your next opportunity! In the words of Maya Angelou, 'If you don't like something, change it. If you can't change it, change your attitude.'[23] Sometimes the smallest shift within us can create a very big impact on others. When stories no longer serve you, it's time to shed them, and you can. You have more strengths and resources than you realise. They need airing and reviewing from time to time. The more you use them, the more choices you have for your impact and influence.

A word on virtual environments

A few years ago, I worked with a group of executives in a global technology company. For them, working remotely, in virtual environments, was the norm, and many of them had never met their bosses face-to-face in all the years they'd worked in the company.

Cut to my world: most (but not all) of my coaching work happens in real time, face-to-face, hands on. In my business, the ability to gauge energy, read body language, observe non-verbal communication and make personal connections is key to getting the data I need in order to serve my clients well.

Cut to somewhere in the middle, where we all live: most of the day-to-day working environments we operate in include remote work and depend on virtual technology: a global conference call spanning different time zones and geographies; Skype, Webex or Zoom meetings; webinars with breakout groups, etc.

In our increasingly technological world, we're enabled by the speed of our connectivity – but we're also seduced by it. Just how connected are we really? (Think about mute buttons, video opt-out, multitasking.)

Here's the thing. Virtual environments require us to be extra vigilant about our presence and our capacity to create engagement. For connectivity to be real, felt and shared in a virtual environment, we must prepare ourselves. And we must be ready to be empathetic.

As well, the zone of the virtual is often cluttered – coffee cups, mouthpieces, screens, headphones, slides, text messages and alerts are just some of the distractions we have to compensate for. Then there's the habitual 'zone of slouch'; we scrunch down into our chairs or hunch over our screens.

The magnificent contradiction of operating in the virtual world is that we have to be more conscious than ever about connecting to our bodies – our first environment – to be present with our audience.

Here's a toolkit for preparing to host in a virtual environment.

VIRTUAL HOST PREPARATION EXERCISE

⊕ **Empathy**: Get grounded and centred. *Stop! and breathe.* Slow yourself down and visualise your audience. Create empathy and curiosity. Imagine the different people in their offices, their homes, in airport lounges or in transit, on smartphones, iPads, laptops, or desktops. Imagine all the different time zones you'll be sharing, the breadth and reach of your collective geography, things that might be going on within those different time zones and settings, the diversity of lives.

⊕ **Appreciation**: Take a moment to appreciate that each person will be turning up, committing time and space to listen, to think and to contribute. Put an imaginary spotlight on your audience and 'see' them (before you actually see them, if you have a visual forum).

⊕ **Connection**: Check in with your audience at the start of the call to acknowledge where they are and how they are. Share a 'humanity' moment!

⊕ **Framing**: Set the scene (why we're here), clarify the objectives (what we're doing) and confirm understanding with everyone before diving into the agenda.

⊕ **Voice**: Speak *slowly* (compensate for all those barriers, zones, languages) and clearly. Take pauses. Let people hear, process, think.

⊕ **Energy**: Stand up on the call to free your voice and be more animated and alert. Create the structure and environment for optimal listening and participation. Maintain your energy and sustain the group's energy.

⊕ **Endings**: Be clear about what the asks, tasks and next steps are. Be sure to acknowledge and appreciate everyone's time. How you end a virtual session is every bit as important as how you begin it.

⊕ **Your ingredient:** Bring into play the unique thing you bring to the table that enables everyone to leave the virtual space feeling it was worthwhile.

'Who has time for all this?' I hear you say. It only takes a minute. And it really pays.

COACH IN YOUR POCKET POINTERS

- Preparing yourself is as important as preparing your content. It's your job to create the environment needed for maximum engagement and results.

- Before rushing into a meeting or other scenario, take a moment to clarify objectives and intentions. Ask yourself, 'What is needed here? How do I need to show up?'

- Apply one of your 'at your best' qualities to a scenario that challenges you.

CHAPTER 6

Powerful Communication Is A Physical Act

*I speak two languages,
Body and English.*[24]

(MAE WEST)

When I attend live performances of theatre, dance or music, my favourite place to be is right up close and personal. I love seeing the human being and the performer. In the business world, the best and most engaging presenters and speakers are those who come out from behind the PowerPoint, who take time to breathe, to look, to see, to pause, and to think. They are in the moment. They are with their audience. Compelling, effective communicators make great things happen.

I find it amusing that communication is often still referred to as a 'soft skill'. For my money, great communication requires a high level of fitness. The 'job' of great communication is to connect, create engagement, build relationships and fuel productivity. The job is to articulate something of value. The job is to create a space for ideas to flourish – a space for buy-in and positive results. The job is to make your words, feelings, energy and passion reach others. Soft skill?

Building relationships with your clients, building trust and motivation with your team, selling an idea or a product, putting yourself forward for a promotion, stepping into a challenging transition, creating a vision or rejuvenating key messages that may have gone unexamined for a while – all these things require an investment in *how* you say what you say (as much as in *what* you say).

When you do that – when you invest in *how* you say what you say – people take notice and want to listen. It ignites their confidence and commitment. More than that, it *inspires them* – and everyone works with a clearer sense of purpose, feels more motivated and steps into a *bigger self* when they feel inspired.

Let's unpack the *how you say what you say* so you can start inspiring yourself and others right now!

The 3 Cs of preparation

Being the professional you are, with experience, credibility, expertise and accountability, you likely put a lot of effort into preparing your content for key presentations, pitches, meetings and speeches. You've got slide decks and handouts and notes. You've done the research, or your trusted assistant or communications team has, and you've put together a draft script.

At some point, though, you need to shift from preparing your content to preparing yourself, and by that I mean your personal connection to what you're talking about.

Preparing yourself is so important that I hope you'll start doing the personal preparation first and the content preparation second. You'll be amazed by how much this pays off. I call this preparation the '3 Cs'. It opens the valve for fresh, stimulating content that will land with your audience.

THE 3 Cs EXERCISE

First C: Connect to yourself

◉ Clarify what really matters to you about your content and the sense of purpose you have about it. Unless your communication is utterly personal, it won't communicate anything at all.

◉ Articulate the results you want in giving this presentation, talk, pitch.

Second C: Connect to your content

◉ Identify what's at the heart of the 'story' in simple, direct language ('Essentially, this is a story about...')

◉ Clarify the key points and message simply and clearly in human speak, not work jargon.

◉ Find an image or metaphor that works with the message and brings the content to life for you: 'Picture this...'; 'This is like...'; 'What I see...'; 'Imagine this...'

Third C: Connect to your environment (your audience and space)

◉ Answer these questions: Who is your audience? What environment will you be in? How do you need to show up?

> ⊕   Clarify why you want your audience to listen
>   and what's in it for them. When they walk out
>   the door, what do you want them to be saying,
>   thinking about, feeling or doing? Be bold and
>   simple. For example, 'I want them to be saying,
>   "*Now* I understand why we're implementing
>   this change!"'

Do your 3 Cs aloud. This way, you'll get immediate feedback on what you're experiencing:

Flow, clarity, traction

or

Blockage, generalisations, vagueness

By working aloud, you'll hear the sound of your voice and will feel the energy in your body. You'll remember your content quickly and take ownership of it. Preparing your 3 Cs is the foundation from which you can build your performance.

True voice

When is the last time you heard your own voice? Many women admit that when they hear a recording of their voice, they feel disappointed. They say things such as 'Is that what I sound like? My voice sounds so quiet'; 'It sounds more nasal than the way I hear it'; and 'Oh, I talk so fast! But it feels like I'm going really slowly'.

Surprising, isn't it? You use your voice as your primary instrument for communication, for speaking up, presenting, pitching, participating in meetings and engaging in all manner of conversations – virtual and in person – and yet it's unfamiliar to you. Perhaps what you're really saying is that it's uninspiring to you.

If this is your experience, it could be because when you walk into the office, you step into your default zone – that mindset, body and voice you habitually slip into that's shaped by your organisational culture. These cultures have their own language, jargon and invisible rules that say, 'This is the way we do things around here.'

Let's leave the office for a moment and go into your *other* life, the one you leave outside the door when you get to work (but which you'll stop doing from now on, right?).

When you read a fairy tale to a child at bedtime, do you rush through it? Do you speak in bullet-point format? Do you stay in one tone, one gear and one key throughout? No! You instinctively put on different voices for the different characters, slow down and create magic and suspense, speak loudly and softly, etc.

When you're finished reading, do you run out of the room as fast as you can? No! You say, 'The end.' You let your story settle on the child and then you say, 'Goodnight.'

When you call your dog from across a field, you whistle and use your special 'dog-calling voice', right? When you watch a live sports event, you probably shout and cheer a lot. And what about those moments of hysterical, cathartic laughter with a friend? Or singing in the shower? Letting rip while driving and listening to your favourite track? What about those moments you insist that your partner listen as you read a passage from the newspaper out loud with righteous indignation or amazement ('You've *got* to hear this!'). Oh, and let's not forget that domestic argument (yes, that *same* old argument again!).

Wow! What a wide-ranging, dynamic, expressive, contoured voice you have, don't you agree? So what happens when you walk through the door of your workplace? Why the big gag over your mouth? That dynamic voice of yours gets damped down, flattened and rushed. You're surfing the monotone airwaves rather than tuning into your bright personal bandwidth.

Please stop this vocal laziness right now.

Your voice is your gateway to your presence, your signature style and your capacity to influence those around you. How do you hear yourself? How do you want to be heard?

It's time to invest in your voice to lift those words off the page, bring them to life and create meaning. Legend has it that the great French chanteuse, Edith

Piaf, talked about being able to sing a phone book and make it sound good; and so can you! And the great news is you don't need a battery of voice training. You've got everything you need to influence, convince and inspire with your voice. How? One word: *intention*.

Intention directs expression

When you have a clear intention regarding *what* you want to say and *why* you want to say it, the *how* aligns accordingly. Your body, voice, energy, breath, belief and expressiveness rally around you.

Energy author Eileen McDargh says, 'When you lose your "why" you lose your "way".'[25] When you remind yourself what really matters to you in your messages, you'll get a surge of confidence, ease and flow. From there, you'll understand what emotional tone you want to project to your audience (the how) because you'll be clear about your objectives (the what). Clarifying your intention is your driver and your traction. Are you talking to your audience in order to:

- Challenge?
- Reassure?
- Motivate?
- Provoke?
- Persuade?
- Inspire?

Jen had a particularly important engagement. She was going to talk to her whole division to celebrate the success of a project, express appreciation for everyone's outstanding work and share the news that they had won a prestigious new contract.

Once Jen clarified for herself that her key message was about 'building on success', she knew she needed to 'uplift, inspire and motivate'. With her emotional and energetic intention clear, Jen had a mandate for her voice: be positive and enthusiastic.

On her personal energy scale, Jen knew she had to hit the 8 to 10 range, so she ramped up accordingly. As she smiled to convey appreciation and celebration, her voice automatically projected warmth and energy.

To 'model' her uplifting message further, she stood taller (no rocking back or standing in a twisted pretzel) and held the group in her sight line with a more open stance. This heightened posture also had a positive impact on her voice projection. As well, she made sure to make genuine eye contact with her audience, to take time to really see them, signalling, 'I like it here with you'.

By clarifying her intentions for this talk ('I want to appreciate, celebrate and motivate'), Jen, not a natural extrovert or bravura performer, was able to make conscious choices about her body language, voice and energy that significantly shifted her performance out of her default to a more inspirational zone. In terms of her energy wardrobe, Jen shed her grey T-shirt and dressed for the part.

Paula had to have a 'critical conversation' – she had to say no to a request and give some strong pushback to her boss about why. She had to clarify for herself that her message had two parts: one part was about the pushback itself ('This is what I *can't* do') and the other part was about maintaining a good, trust-based relationship with her boss ('This is what I *can* do').

Emotionally and energetically, Paula clarified her intention: to be unapologetic and firm and also positive and explorative. Paula knew she had to ground herself, take her time and be honest and real.

Rushing and sounding tentative or negative were the pitfalls she had to avoid. To model respectful pushback rather than jumping through hoops, Paula knew she had to invest in relaxation, clarity and gravitas.

As you can see, these two scenarios required different kinds of voices, expressions and energy. They were both authentic 'performances' that considered a palette of possibilities, which became available as soon as Jen and Paula clarified their intentions. *Remember, intention directs expression.*

Setting clear intentions regarding what you're talking about and why you're talking about it will reveal the feeling and energy you need to invest. This will send a powerful message to your intuitive body and voice to express itself accordingly. So listen up, and once more with feeling!

Warm up the instrument

Singers and musicians warm up with scales. Dancers and athletes stretch their muscles. As all great performers and athletes know, you have to warm up the instrument. Skipping warm-ups results in lacklustre performances. It's as simple as that.

Remember, you are an executive athlete! Did you really think you could go in cold? Communication is a physical act. It involves your body, voice, breath, energy and belief. It requires your full presence. It demands clear intentions and getting into the right state. You need to *tune up* before you *turn up*!

The great news is, it's really easy. Deep breaths, stretching tall with your arms overhead, running in place, reading or speaking a few lines of something inspirational out loud at increasing volume and clapping vigorously (your own standing ovation!) are all fast and effective ways to warm yourself up, raise your energy levels, enhance your articulation and put you into a positive state.

It really is that simple. Enjoy creating your own warm-ups. Do something; do anything! But from this day forward, *do not* go into that important communication moment cold.

WARM UP EXERCISES

◉ While standing, scrunch over and make yourself as small and closed as possible. Slowly, over ten counts, unfurl; stretch up and up your spine into an uplifted posture until your arms are high, your face is lifted to the sky and your face muscles are stretched into a huge (forced) smile. Then reverse it all and scrunch over again.

◉ Stretch your arms up and make a big, audible yawn. Really make some noise! Let your vocal cords open.

◉ Do energy scales (1, 5, 10): Speak aloud one simple statement, eg 'This is a beautiful room', or 'Hi, it's great to be here!' Speak it at level-1 energy and volume, then level-5 energy and volume, then level-10 energy and volume. Notice how your body and voice come into play at each investment level.

You are audience and performer

Think of the last time you went to the theatre, the cinema, a concert, a dance performance or any other event where you were in the role of audience. Were you spellbound? Enthralled? Amused? Confused? Nodding off? Did you arrive at the event exhausted but obliged to attend? Were you looking forward to it?

When we're in the role of audience, inside or outside the workplace, we are first and foremost human beings, carrying our circumstances with us. There is no such thing as a generalised 'them' – ie 'the audience', 'one big block', or, to use the phobic boardroom term, 'the enemy'. We audiences are human beings who have come from somewhere to get here, to the event. As audience, we have committed time and effort. We want to be engaged and inspired! We want the performer to succeed.

All of us are playing either the role of audience or the role of performer. We speak or we listen. We view or we do. We want to give something or we want to get something. That's the contract.

Think again about yourself when you're in the role of audience. Which performers inspire you and what are some of their qualities? Perhaps:

- Being real

- Good storytelling

- Well-judged pace and projection

- Dynamic body language

- Eye contact that makes you feel as if you have the speaker's undivided attention

- Clarity and accessibility

- Levity

These are some of the qualities we notice when we're in the role of audience. So steal them and steal well! Make the very things that inspire you about others part of your authentic way of performing.

Take the spotlight off you and your anxieties ('Will I remember all my points?'; 'I wish I'd had more time to prepare') and mentally put the spotlight on your audience. In other words, it's not about you, it's about them! Be interested in them. See them. Appreciate them. Be real with them. Play the role of hostess at a dinner party and look after them. Don't lobotomise your content into data! Information downloads don't cut it. *Think 'perform' not 'inform'.*

Boardroom tables are performance spaces

Oh habits! Habits! Why does the act of sitting around a boardroom table give you permission to collapse, withdraw, become smaller, shrink your visibility and make less impact with your voice? I know you don't intend to, and I know you know better. But it happens time and again. Consider these two scenarios.

1. You're rushing from meeting to meeting and not taking that precious, critical breathing space to clear your brain, clarify your intention and refresh your energy for your next environment. Instead of taking a moment to prepare yourself consciously, you throw

yourself into the room, launch into 'organise-as-you-go' mode and get through as best you can.

2. At the beginning of a meeting you're mindful of your body language, attentiveness and engagement, but as it progresses, you gradually forget and lapse into the habitual zone of less-than-full-investment of your presence. Things start to slip as you start multitasking, or mentally withdrawing, or not speaking up and forfeiting your moment or idea (which someone else takes over).

Please remember that a boardroom table is a stage. You just happen to be sitting down.

Imagine the table under a spotlight on a stage. Go big and theatrical with me for a moment. Stand back and see the scene as if watching a movie. What choices for impact do you have?

- Where do you choose to sit?

- When do you sit tall?

- Lean forward?

- Make eye contact around the table?

- Pause for presence?

- Speak up?

- Place your hands on the table to make a point?

- Sit back and take in the whole group at once?

- Ask a question?

- Ask for something to be repeated or repeat a point yourself?

- Take a moment to refresh your energy by changing your posture?

- Show that you're listening?

The boardroom table – ie the meeting-room environment – is likely to be your most frequently inhabited performance space. I'll say that again. You probably spend more time in the meeting-room environment than anywhere else in your day. If this is true, then it's the environment you need to enliven for yourself and for others as much as possible.

Starting right now, change your boardroom environment from being an energy drainer to an energy booster. Wear every piece from your energy wardrobe. Enjoy making choices for impact and start tracking the results.

Beginnings

In every presentation course I've ever led, and I mean *every* one, the big barrier is this: beginnings. The beginnings of most talks or presentations are pretty dull, agreed?

Imagine speaking to your audience as if they were one person and you were shaking hands with them. In a positive, meaningful encounter with another person, you wouldn't snatch your hand away instantly after a handshake. You would make eye contact and hold the moment as you exchanged greetings. Speaking to your audience is like that handshake: turn up, be real, be interested and connect.

Let's explore these beginnings a little further. Here's a scenario you might have experienced yourself: Everyone is seated around a table. At one end of the room is a flip chart or a PowerPoint set-up. Perhaps you're up first. Perhaps you're number six up to speak. Whatever your slot, it's your moment. You're on!

There's silence as you get out of your chair and walk to your spot. You just want to get this over with, and your body language is a dead giveaway.

You are in the throes of your *death walk* – that zone of complete disconnect from yourself, your environment and your audience. During the death walk, whether it's one foot or ten yards, you're temporarily 'offline', in a bubble of paralysis or self-absorption.

Suddenly, as if controlled by a master puppeteer in an alternate universe, you snap into 'presentation mode', starting with the usual box-ticking niceties (while avoiding direct eye contact) or clichéd conventions (eg 'tell them what you're going to tell them, then tell them'). That moment of disconnect, feeling the glare of the spotlight on you, makes for very heavy lifting!

About two minutes in, you're warming up and hitting a respectable stride. But in stage time, two minutes is a long time. You need to be warmed up from the start. You need to be present, real and engaged from the start.

Ever do the 'hook' test when deciding which book to read on your holiday? Out of your three possible choices, you read the first paragraph in each and whichever book hooks you in that first paragraph wins. That's your holiday reading sorted! It works the same way with television programmes or films. How long do you give that Season 1, Episode 1 before you either commit or continue surfing?

Presentations need to hook from the start too. You need to be warmed up to yourself, to your subject and to your audience from the start, connected from the start. In the theatre, actors warm up offstage. Frequently they begin their scenes in the wings and come on stage animated, full of life and already 'in' the story.

To avoid the death walk, *start from where you are!* Yes. Your presentation starts from where you're sitting. Your seat is your launch pad. You're already there, at the table, in contact with everyone around you, seeing them and hearing them. Use all this environmental 'data' to be in the moment. Use the chair as your base from which to get grounded and from which to lift off.

Choose your moment. It's your show. Own it. Now rise from the chair *with intention* and start speaking. All that connection, that ease, that conscious choice is with you, and it's reassuring for your audience. We're hooked from the start because you've started! No dead space, no fillers, no artificial switch into presentation mode.

ENERGETIC LAUNCH
EXERCISE

Try this ABA sequence as a practice tool:

A: Begin speaking your presentation in your chair at the table. Look at the people around the table as you begin (I know you're trying this alone, so use your imagination).

B: Gradually get to your feet – keep speaking – start walking – keep speaking – and arrive at your desired spot – keep speaking. The walk itself will force you to breathe and change your energy.

A: As you wrap up your presentation, walk back to your chair and sit down but stay energised and connected with your audience around the table.

Using the ABA format will keep you connected to your audience, will help you feel at ease and real in the moment, and will loosen you up.

Even if you don't do this in your actual presentations, it's a great practice tool for giving you natural momentum and flow.

The scintillation of distillation

When I was an academic supervising PhD students, I often struggled to understand what their theses were. In their quest to contribute to 'original knowledge', the students opted for complexity over clarity. So I introduced a method in my supervision which required the radical distillation of each thesis into a sentence or two, max. My belief was that if they couldn't describe their research in a sentence or two, they didn't have a thesis.

I still subscribe to this idea, and nowhere is it more brilliantly applied than in show biz. According to Broadway lore, the musical *Fiddler on the Roof,* which opened in 1964 and went on to become the longest-running show in history, went through countless drafts among the show's creative team. In a game-changing meeting, the choreographer-director Jerome Robbins asked the team again and again and again what the show was *really* about. Finally, the lyricist Sheldon Harnick blurted out, 'It's about tradition.' The rest is history.[26]

Now think of movies – the dark dramas, the adventures of heroes, the twist-a-minute thrillers, the moral dilemmas, and the romantic comedies. Their promotional blurbs are only a sentence and yet they grab the heart of the story. For example, 'A gripping coming-of-age tale about three boys who witness a murder and vow their silence.' See what I mean?

Radical distillation is one of the best tools in the toolkit for getting right to the heart of what you're talking about.

RADICAL DISTILLATION EXERCISE

- ⊕ Speak for a couple of minutes about your subject. No need for a script, just ad-lib. Set a timer for three minutes, max.

- ⊕ Now distil that content into three complete sentences, each with a full stop (no cheating with run-ons using lots of 'ands'!).

- ⊕ Finally, distil your three sentences into three words. *Make each word matter.* Think of each word as a gateway to a whole presentation. Imagine each word as a flag and physically enact 'planting' it in the ground, or imagine each word as a billboard and enact holding up the billboard.

- ⊕ Notice how these key words act as an anchor for you and give you traction and clarity regarding what your story is really 'about'.

Nothing is more scintillating for an audience than bold, clear simplicity, which gives them access to your ideas and invites them on board.

Get to the point

Recently, while working on puzzles with my three-year-old granddaughter in Vancouver, I spent too long sorting the pieces into piles. As a result, my granddaughter wandered off, her puzzle enthusiasm fizzled out and her focus already elsewhere. And who could blame her? She wanted to make a puzzle but it took too long to get to the good bit!

It's the same for presentations. You need to turbocharge those beginnings, get stuck in and get to the point! Cease and desist from convoluted conventions, endless framing and lengthy introductions. Create an energetic launch and get to the good stuff as soon as possible.

There are no rules, just conscious decisions

I once attended a talk in an auditorium designed for two hundred or more people, but at which only two people turned up, including me.

Astonishingly, the presenter stuck to his script and to his rehearsed delivery style, geared towards a full auditorium. Setting aside the possibility that the talk was being recorded and therefore it was necessary to perform it as originally planned, it was very awkward to witness a 'big house' formal lecture to an audience of two!

I would have preferred it by far had the speaker sat on the edge of the stage, torn up the script and changed gear completely. I'll bet you can think of a presentation or pitch where someone stayed on script no matter what. Presentation training, with its often stilted playbook, has a lot to answer for. 'Rules' such as 'Tell them what you're going to tell them, then tell them, then tell them what you told them' and 'Touch the tips of your fingers together in front of you to show gravitas' should be banished!

The only rule you ever need to know is called 'Make it a conscious decision'.

- When to move and when to be still: Unconscious, constant moving around is distracting. Consciously deciding when to move and when to be still is compelling. There are lots of choices – sitting down, standing up, moving closer to your audience, moving further back, crossing to one side of the room and then the other. These are all good choices in using space as long as they're done consciously, to get your message across.

- Gestures: a hand in a pocket, a hand gesture, hands clasped, and arms out and open are all good choices as long as they're done consciously, help make your points *and bring you and your subject to life.*

- There's no need to stay stuck in one mode. Do what frees you and best supports you in the moment so you can be real and be connected to your audience.

Slick, pat, rehearsed performances that stick to the script and the delivery style *no matter what* are not alive. They're all about 'getting the job done' and nothing about taking care of your audience. These kinds of performances may convey critical information, but they'll leave audiences cold.

Flexibility, adaptability, thinking on your feet and making conscious decisions in the moment are key to connecting with your audience, keeping it real and authentic and landing your messages. In the words of the late, great choreographer Pina Bausch, 'I'm not interested in how people move, but what moves them.'[27]

The best practice tool to achieve this skill in no time is to put your script and slides to one side and ad-lib.

- Try a three-minute version, a two-minute version and a one-minute version.

- Try delivering sitting down, standing up and a combination of both.

- Enjoy exploring this – treat it like circuit training! It's great for agility and clarity and for revealing instantly what kind of choices for impact you can make.

Remember, if it's a conscious choice, it's the right choice.

Endings

According to music lore Bo Diddley once said, 'I thank you in advance for the great round of applause I'm about to get.' Marvellous! I urge you all to use this as your mantra before speaking to an audience.

In presentation and public-speaking workshops, I often set the following challenge for participants: 'At the end of your delivery, stay put and look at your audience while they applaud.' Given the pain evident in their facial expressions and body language, you would be forgiven for thinking that the participants were literally having their feet held to the flame.

Applause, like compliments, praise or positive feedback, seems to be another one of those gifts that gets routinely dodged and dropped to the ground rather than received with appreciation. Let's take a moment to reframe this shoddy, habitual attitude.

The *end* of a presentation (cue applause or appreciative, thoughtful silence) is the *beginning* of a relationship with your audience. Applause doesn't just signal 'thank you' – applause is also real energy created in the human connection that's been forged. Now the next conversations can truly begin, from that connection, and your objectives in showing up and presenting can manifest.

The 'Thank you for coming' at the start and the 'Thank you for listening' at the end are bookends that show you value your audience. Their applause, in turn, shows they value you.

Keep these reframes in mind while I describe the shocking behaviours I witness more often than not when speakers are finishing a performance:

- I see them shut down while still 'on', their eyes to the carpet, their connection with their audience broken, their posture collapsed.

- I see them rush out of the space, signalling, 'Phew! Over and done with!'

- I see post-mortems (eg a wince and apologetic body language for taking up time).

- I see endings that speed up, with last sentences dropping through the floor and key messages dissolving into a mumbled, anticlimactic, forgettable non-ending.

How insulting! Did you ever consider the effect of this disappearing act on your audience? And what if you pulled this stunt when your audience was giving you the gift of applause? Shame on you, dodging that gift of appreciation and attention!

So hold your horses. Stay right where you are and let's try this once more with feeling: Breathe, stand still, look at your audience, wait a beat... OK. *Now* you can let go of that metaphorical handshake. But oh! There you go again, rushing off and disconnecting just because you've finished speaking. Stay in the now. Keep the connection with your audience. Now is not the time for a post-mortem. Keep the energy of the environment alive – you, your audience, the ideas, the listening. Be that good host of your own dinner party and take care of your guests, the audience. Everything should signal 'Welcome to this meeting ground'.

COACH IN YOUR POCKET POINTERS

- ⊕ Set clear intentions for why you're speaking and what you want your audience to experience.

- ⊕ Distil your content.

- ⊕ Warm up.

- ⊕ Slow down and take pauses when speaking.

- ⊕ Mentally put the spotlight on your audience and be interested in them!

- ⊕ Make conscious decisions about your beginnings, your movements and your endings.

CHAPTER 7

Great Performers Rehearse

*When I miss class for one day,
I know it. When I miss class for
two days, the teacher knows it.
When I miss class for three days,
the audience knows it.*[28]

(RUDOLF NUREYEV)

All great performers rehearse, and that includes you. Rehearsal is space and time for practising and improving the impact you want to make on yourself and others – your audience, team, stakeholders and organisation. The better it's rehearsed, the better the performance. The better the performance, the more buy-in. Rehearsal is profit.

In its simplest sense, rehearsal is doing. It is action. It is experiential. Consider the well-known maxim about learning: 'I hear and I forget. I see and I remember. I do and I understand.'

In the act of rehearsal, you embody 'doing' with your whole self: body, mind, emotion, imagination, voice, energy and purpose. This is a profoundly different process from merely reading through notes or thinking through something in your head or repeating something over and over to memorise, polish or perfect.

When you take a bit of time to rehearse out loud, rehearse physically, and rehearse creatively by trying things out, you are mightily rewarded: You make discoveries, and you break through limiting habits. You upgrade your performance.

In my years as a professional theatre director and choreographer, the rehearsal room was (and remains) my favourite space. Like a scientist's lab, it's a place for experimenting, exploring and discovering. Often the most powerful and poignant moments show up in rehearsal by accident. We allow ourselves to fail and fail again, but 'fail better', as Samuel Beckett says,[29] because we can. The rehearsal room is a safe haven where you can dare to take risks.

Rehearsals are a liberating opportunity to tear up your script and dig a little deeper; to generate new ideas, new thinking and new material. This is the time and space where you can revitalise your vision, your messages and your self.

So practise but don't lock it down right away! The art of rehearsal can truly cultivate your creativity and confidence and grow your performance.

Lisa, from a medical research organisation, was invited to give a TEDx talk. She spent several weeks crafting her story, assembling visuals and practising as often as possible. About a week before the event, Lisa asked me to help her rehearse.

She was word-perfect, but her data had no soul. Lisa wasn't connecting personally to her story; she wasn't speaking from her heart. Her content was well structured and substantial and contained some life-affirming messages. But all the good bits were buried under the *how* of her delivery.

Radical-action alert! The stuff rehearsals are made for. I asked Lisa to put her script back in her briefcase and begin again without it. I asked her to slow down, *really slow down*, and to paraphrase each unit of her story, talk to me about her feelings and notice what her body was doing.

Lisa gamely plotted her way through. There were tears. There was laughter. There was playfulness and even a bit of singing. Through rehearsal, Lisa was able to take ownership of her story, show her vulnerability and humanity and embody her messages. She took hold of that axe of Kafka's and broke through the ice of the 'frozen sea' within her.

When she practised it again after this exploration, the performance was so nuanced and alive! More importantly, Lisa had discovered another aspect of rehearsal that was vital for her performance growth – *connecting to herself.* Her talk inspired the hundreds of women who were in the audience that day.

In its best form, a rehearsal is a process through which you connect powerfully, truthfully and deeply to yourself and experience energy, flow and fearless creative fire. Your unique life force is set free.

Fall in love with language

Poetry, songs, great speeches, literature – anything in the world of words that inspires you – helps you to fall in love with language. For a little while, you step into the realm of the extraordinary. For a little while, your body, voice and emotions are uplifted. For a little while, you connect with the performer within. When you speak words that inspire you, you are more playful, daring, and courageous. You take your moment to be heard. You hear yourself differently.

Cut to the world of work: Language is PowerPoint presentations, bullet-point agendas, company acronyms and corporate jargon. Messages are often pat, slick and repeated. After a while, it's hard to hear the words you're speaking habitually much less maintain a living, vital sense of what they mean, why they're important or what matters to you about saying them.

Speaking language that is extraordinary in some way, heightened beyond the everyday, wakes us up to the power of words to influence, inspire or illuminate. Start now. Find a poem, song lyrics or speech you love and read the words out loud as a warm-up to energise your voice, inspire your imagination and ignite your love of language. Speak as if you're speaking about ideas, not just reciting words.

Now return to one of your workplace messages and do exactly what you just did with your inspirational text:

- Speak the thoughts and ideas – don't just recite the words

- Give the words space and air by pausing

- Walk towards what you're saying; don't back away from your words

- Keep your animated, inspired energy alive

- Speak your work messages as if they are magnificent

Work out loud and on purpose

I've lost count of how many times I've said this thing about working out loud, but it's so important that I'll probably say it a few more times along the way. It's a foolproof litmus test of how you value what you're talking about.

When you rehearse out loud:

- You get immediate feedback on your alignment with your messages, an ecology check.

- You notice the bits you're struggling with, those phrases that get strangled in your throat because they're too complicated (words that obscure rather than enable meaning and understanding).

- You commit to your ideas more convincingly (or not) because your whole body is involved and, in the words of the great dance pioneer, Martha Graham 'the body never lies'.[30]

- You remember your material more quickly. Speaking out loud and embodying (standing up, moving around, pausing, breathing, gesturing) triggers your memory. It's a fast track to being able to go off script, think on your feet and deliver your messages in different ways for different audiences.

- You keep the content fresh for yourself and therefore more interesting. And if *you* are interested in your messages, your audiences will be too!

Play it big

One of my modern-dance teachers, the late and great Joyce Trisler, always said, 'If you make a mistake, make it big.' She meant that we need to commit wholeheartedly, not tentatively. Only when you commit and work big do you see clearly and understand what needs to happen. By working big, you physically step into your thinking. You feel, sense, see, hear, embody, and go with your gut and heart. Reading silently through your notes while sitting at your desk just doesn't cut it.

Think of the last time you came across a passage, quote or piece of data you wanted to capture. Chances are you highlighted that bit. Perhaps you underline key points in red on your 'to do' list or when editing a document. We use underlining and highlighting to capture, pay special attention to, recall and remember.

Exaggeration is the embodied, physical equivalent of using that highlighter pen. By exaggerating things, we can capture our awareness just like we capture data with the highlighter pen.

Think about your last meet-and-greet; perhaps you were at a networking event or just meeting a new colleague for the first time. No doubt you politely shook hands and smiled, made eye contact and said something like 'pleased to meet you'. It's likely you did this naturally and without much effort (even if you hate networking or are shy meeting people you don't know).

Now imagine yourself at the airport about to reunite with a loved one you haven't seen for a long time and have missed terribly. You're there at the gate ready to meet them. You see each other and run towards each other and... well, it's *your* story. You finish it! Whatever you see in this scenario, though, it isn't likely to involve a handshake (personally, I'm seeing bear hugs and squeals of excitement or even tears). Whatever your version looks like, it doesn't look the same as your meet-and-greet moment in the workplace, right?

By exaggerating and playing it big, you instantly reveal your huge range of energy and expressiveness, from more contained and neutral (your workplace handshake) to heightened and highly charged (your reunion at the airport).

Exaggeration is a magnificent tool for *building your range of dynamics and expressiveness*. Here's a quick and effective exaggeration exercise to try right now.

EXAGGERATION
EXERCISE

⊙   Find something that attracts your attention.
     It can be anything from a sign to a socket, a
     painting to a ventilation fan – anything you
     notice, however mundane or mysterious.

⊙   Now imagine you're holding a magic
     wand and with one flick of it – *Swish!* –
     you transform that object into the most
     extraordinary thing you've ever seen.

Staying in this realm of the magical, describe
this object using words that befit something
that is the most extraordinary thing you've ever
seen (yes, close your door for this one). I'll bet
you sounded very different from your usual self
when you did this, and I'll bet your body language
ramped up too. Hopefully, you've discovered in
an instant what a big range of vocal dynamism
you have – you just need to remember to use it!

Exaggeration helps us to remember what we
already know deep inside but have forgotten; it is
simply dormant.

Improvise and be surprised

On a rainy day in Dublin many years ago, I arrived at the studio theatre where I was directing a production, ready to rehearse with the cast for the press preview the following night. I loved working with this ensemble of talented young actors, and I was excited about the originality of the show we had created together. I felt the usual anticipation and buzz.

Oddly, the door to the theatre was unlocked, so I figured one of the technicians had already arrived. But it was dark inside. Something was wrong. I turned on the lights. The shock of what I saw made me cry out. The theatre had been vandalised. All the sets and costumes were destroyed. Everything was ruined. I just sat there, numb. A few minutes later the cast arrived and joined in the shock and horror. Thoroughly dismayed, we were stopped in our tracks.

After a few minutes of processing the catastrophe before us, something kicked in: a determination to fight back with all our humanity and creativity. We had worked for two months pretty much 24/7 on this production, and through our intensive rehearsal process we had become a family, connected through trust, reliability and teamwork of the highest order.

We were going to have to improvise our way out of this mess.

So here was my plan:

Step 1 - Clear all the debris and make the space a fresh slate, a clean space without the reminder of the vandalism.

Step 2 - Get agreement from the ensemble, the team, that we would commit 100% to carrying on and getting the show up.

Step 3 - Inspire and motivate every performer to believe in their talent and experience and envision what we could create anew.

It was a very long day and a very long night. By the next morning, we had created a 'poor man's theatre', which was lean but exciting. Without props, costumes or sets, this radically stripped-down production offered a brave, unapologetic, intentional form of storytelling. The performers acted as if this bare-bones style was their magical USP. Not only did the show get great reviews, it had an extended run!

Improvisation is the art of transforming uncertainty into new possibilities. It can be a liberating opportunity to tear up the script, the plan, the blueprint and take a risk, take action and find creative solutions – something new.

You are a master improvisor

We're often terrified by the idea of being unprepared or unscripted, of ad-libbing or taking a step into the unknown. Yet we're all highly experienced improvisors in our everyday lives.

I'll bet you can recall a time something went wrong and you improvised your way through. Perhaps you were about to give a presentation only to discover your notes were missing or PowerPoint wasn't working. Somehow you gave that presentation and the sky didn't fall in just because things didn't go to plan.

Maybe the improvised version of your presentation was more alive, more memorable than the one you'd planned! A scary experience but an exhilarating lesson as well. You might have forgotten some of your points, but the audience didn't know the script – they were engaging with *you*.

What about that speech you gave that came from your heart spontaneously at a wedding or birthday celebration? Or the time you sat in awe as you listened to a friend strum a new piece of music into existence on a guitar, right there and then? Remember suddenly having a flash of inspiration and jotting down the poem that poured effortlessly onto the page? Or that think-tank session where you and your team did some fearless blue-sky thinking, throwing out as many ideas as possible in a short amount of time? What about those occasions when you made up a story on the spot for a child instead of reading one?

Overthinking an action can create more fear and anxiety in us than actually performing the action. Adrenaline and vulnerability are with all of us when we step into the unknown and the unscripted. But with practice, your improvisational muscles get fitter and stronger and fear becomes a more productive form of excitement.

The more we practise something, the more fluent we become in it and the more confident we become doing it, and that includes improvisation. Stand-up comedians make a great study in practised spontaneity as they play off their audience, volley with hecklers and customise their set to their audience's location and culture. It seems like a contradiction: how can you practise being in the zone of the unknown?

What you're practising when you improvise is being completely present with others. It builds trust, courage and confidence like nothing else. Leaders today have to embrace change and navigate ambiguity. To do so successfully requires optimism, curiosity and agility. The practice of improvisation increases your fitness levels for these challenges.

By shaking things up, you grant yourself the freedom to act with what you have – see what happens; learn something, interact with people in unpredictable ways, adjust how you do things. We all benefit from sometimes replacing best-laid plans with spontaneous action. We don't always need a blueprint. Sometimes we just need to call 'Action!' and jump right in.

IMPROVISATION EXERCISE

If you're currently working on a presentation, talk or pitch, or if you want to revitalise something you've been delivering for a while, try this improvisation exercise.

- ⊕ Set your timer and improvise for at least two minutes without your notes and see what new ideas and thoughts come up. You'll probably discover that you have many more interesting things to say than you thought.

- ⊕ Free-associate or riff on key words that are important anchors for your content.

- ⊕ Find some images that resonate with your key ideas, drivers or messages and use them as triggers to capture your thoughts and fresh language.

- ⊕ Pick some random objects and have fun making as many 'forced' connections between the object and your subject as you can. For example, 'This glass of water is like the next phase of growth in our sector because...'

You'll be surprised to discover how imaginative you are under a bit of playful pressure!

Your performance is alive, not preserved

When PowerPoint slide decks become a crutch or when a script is so locked down it's practically mummified, it's time for a fresh approach to structuring – one that gives you more freedom and spontaneity. Structure is a great road map and organiser but it doesn't keep your content fresh and alive.

You need to be agile enough with your content to adapt to different environments and audiences. Your content is always a story about something (even if it's numbers!). And since you're the one telling that story, you're the artistic director. You get to decide how your audience hears that story; you get to decide how to create maximum impact and engagement. You'll want to be able to remember your content easily to free yourself from notes.

A dynamic storyboard is your fast-track rehearsal tool for this. It allows you to physicalise your content. The link between movement and memory dates back to the ancient art of loci, or the 'memory palace technique'. Moving to different locations and associating key moments in the story with different images, objects or enactments is like a neurological supercharge. You embody your story, and in turn, it's stored in your body memory.

TEMPLATE:
DYNAMIC STORYBOARD
Title of Story

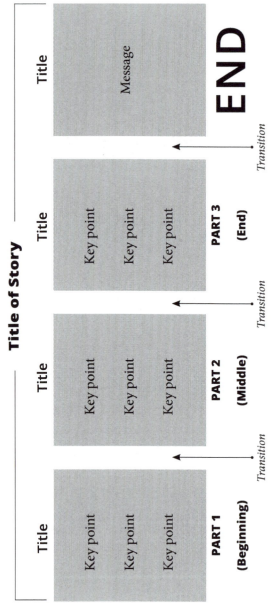

You can download a larger version of this template by going to *www.theatre4business.com* and clicking on the Performing As YOU resources link on the website.

- Map out your story in three boxes for the classic beginning, middle and end structure or, if you prefer, Part 1, Part 2 and Part 3. Create a separate box for your key message and ending.

- Across the top of your boxes give the whole story a title.

- Next, imagine that each box of your story (Parts 1, 2 and 3) is a story in itself, and give each box a title.

- In each box, note the key points that are essential for that part of the story.

- *Work big* (need it be said?). Use a whiteboard, flip-chart paper or anything that involves standing up and working as big and as physically as possible. Remember, it's a *dynamic* storyboard.

- Walk and talk (aloud) your way through each unit of your storyboard.

- Notice how your story changes from section to section. These changes signal 'gear shifts'. You wouldn't drive in just one gear, would you? Likewise, in telling your story, you need to shift your pace, tone, body language and energy.

- Transitions are the spaces between the boxes. Pay attention to how you sustain your energy from section to section. It helps to move from one spot to another to highlight the transitions.

- Remember, the ending is the last thing your audience takes away. 'Hold' your last word and moment for a few beats to let your message land. Have a clear intention for what you want your audience to think about, feel or do.

Once you know your story and how you want to tell it, this dynamic storyboard will give you the agility and confidence to expand or contract it for different contexts and different audiences.

You can download a bigger version of the dynamic story-board template by going to *www.theatre4business.com* and clicking the Performing As YOU resources link on the website.

Seven top tips for rehearsing

1. **Reading aloud**. When you have a draft ready, always read your work aloud. This practice helps you to immediately identify what needs attention. When you read aloud, you can hear the pace, emphasis, rhythm, clarity and colour of your words. You can get a feel for the sequence and structure of your material.

2. **Dynamic storyboarding**. Every story has a beginning, a middle and an end. Physically map these transitions in your presentation by moving to a different spot for each section. Use each pause as an opportunity to change the tone of your voice, renew your energy and make eye contact with your audience. Take your time.

3. **Tactics**. Explore different intentions with your material. Try delivering your presentation as if to agitate, as if to inspire, as if to challenge, as if to reassure, and so on. Really play with different qualities to colour and stretch your voice and dynamics.

4. **Creative strategies**. What's the first thing your audience will experience? Explore a range of strategies for starting your presentation: ask your audience a question, paint a picture for them to imagine ('Picture this'), make a provocative statement, begin with silence and stillness, tell a story, etc. See how these strategies impact on your material and inform your performance.

5. **Near and far**. Experiment with your presentation in different settings and contexts. See what happens with your energy, voice, pace and passion when you play your presentation 'as if' on an epic scale

(large auditorium) and on an intimate scale (across a table).

6. **Points of view.** Anticipate some questions from the audience. What other perspectives might there be on your material? Enjoy asking some 'off the wall' questions of yourself! Surprise yourself.

7. **Visualisation.** Mentally rehearse by visualising how you want to be seen and heard.

COACH IN YOUR POCKET POINTERS

⊙ Work aloud, work big and move!

⊙ Don't lock it down too soon –
   ad-lib and improvise to generate
   fresh ideas and language.

⊙ Use a dynamic storyboard to
   structure your content and enliven
   your performance.

CHAPTER 8

Ask For
Help

It takes a village.[31]

(HILLARY CLINTON)

Before the days of satellite navigation (GPS), one of the most commonly satirised scenarios was the couple in a car lost and needing help. The woman's solution was to ask a passer-by for directions. The man's response was nothing short of teeth-gritting resistance and a determination to carry on no matter what: no one's help needed, thank you very much!

Hours later, they're still lost. Utterly fed up, the woman shouts out to a passer-by for directions and, presto – they arrive at their destination in minutes.

GPS may have altered the course of many a map-reading argument, but a resistance to asking for help has somehow bedded down in reverse in working life. Women often seem more hesitant than men about asking for what they need and asking for help.

Here are some examples:

- You could do with a more strategic leveraging of contacts in your network.

- You need to reach for the stars and get a powerful influencer, sponsor or advocate.

- The time is right to make that call to your old boss – the one you haven't talked to in a few years but who would be the perfect advisor for you right now.

- You could really benefit from more support to get through a big learning curve.

- You want to get buy-in for your proposal, so you need to create some allies.

- You need fresh ears and eyes to give you a new perspective on a challenge you're facing.

- You want to practise a new skill and need some feedback from a trusted buddy so you can track results.

- You want to go forward for that promotion.

You may recognise some of these scenarios or have scenarios of your own – *the scenarios where you know you could do with help but haven't asked.*

Asking for help shows great strength, and it yields dividends. Earlier, we looked at the habit of damping down emotions for fear of appearing weak. We also saw the power and impact of those who can display their humanity, who can be moved, passionate, emotional and vulnerable without losing their integrity or authority. Those who ask for help also display humanity and integrity.

Think of any project, instance of problem-solving, vision or challenging deliverable and you'll find some form of collaboration at the heart of it. Asking for help so often ignites creative collaboration. And along the way, you build a rich network of people resources.

Your tribe of wise ones

I grew up in a suburb of New York City and spent every waking moment immersed in ballet, modern dance and jazz. When I wasn't dancing, I was watching dance – from classical to musicals to the avant-garde, or I was reading every book on dance I could get my hands on, or I was trying to write about dance. Dance was my diet.

The unlikely part of this story (but I promise you it's true) is that when I was fifteen years old, I decided I wanted to be the dance critic for the *New York Times*. What kind of fifteen-year-old aspires to that? I know. Go figure!

The plot thickens. It's the mid-1960s. The maker and breaker of the dance world and all of Broadway is the *New York Times*'s dance and theatre critic Clive Barnes. Unbeknownst to Mr Barnes, fifteen-year-old me was secretly writing away, a formidable critic's voice in the making.

One Saturday morning, eating pancakes with my father, I let slip my secret aspiration. Without missing a beat, my father said, 'If you want to be a dance critic, learn from the best. Go and see Clive Barnes and show him your writing.'

It would take far more pages than I have space for to describe the catalogue of my reactions to my father's suggestion, but the words 'NO WAY' pretty much nail it.

After patiently listening to said catalogue of protestations, my father replied, 'He's just a human being. Go call him.'

Since you've hung in here, you deserve to know how this story ends. Fifteen-year-old me called the maker and breaker of Broadway and requested an audience.

Result: not only did Clive Barnes invite me to his apartment for a chat and a read-through of at least half a dozen of my reviews, he also made me a bacon, lettuce and tomato sandwich on rye!

Outcome 1: His feedback was 'Good for you! Nice work. Keep practising for the next ten years and you'll be a dance critic.' And I did indeed end up working as a dance critic and arts correspondent for several fulfilling years.

Outcome 2: My father, from that moment, became a role model and wise one regarding self-belief and self-worth. In his view, rank and status, titles and positions, were only as good as the humanity behind them and within them.

His absolute conviction was that I had every right and opportunity to reach for the stars, to hope for receptivity but not fear rejection, to admire my icons but not lose sight of my own value. My father remained a key wise one throughout my life and career, offering perspective and challenges at many critical junctures.

To this day, I've benefitted from that experience, and I've enjoyed dialogue, interviews and inspirational conversation with the great, good and famous. There's no time for stage fright when you encounter your hero or heroine! Imagine what you could learn.

Role models inspire our life stories and are a powerful resource when we face challenges, decisions, critical uncertainty and defining moments in our lives. You'll need them, and they'll be there for you when you do, but their voices may be faint and almost forgotten. So search them out and recall their wisdom to shore yourself up when you need to.

THREE MESSAGES EXERCISE

- ◉ Think about three key figures in your life who were/are inspirational, supportive, loyal advocates: Your invincible grandmother? A teacher who saw your potential? A boss who threw you into the deep end?

  Don't overthink it! Work from the gut and the heart. Hone in on the specific quality or attribute that inspires/inspired you about this figure.

You can do this next bit physically, as it's suggested here, or you can just sit and reflect.

Write each name *big* (yup, work big) on a separate piece of paper. Then place each name on the floor spaced well apart and directly ahead of you, like a path of stepping stones.

⊙ Step up to the first name and state your challenge/question out loud. Then ask your wise one: 'What is your message to me?' Capture the first thing you hear and speak it out loud. Walk to your second role model and repeat the sequence. Walk to your third role model and repeat the sequence.

⊙ Sit and write or reflect on the three messages you received from your three wise ones. What did they offer you and how does it help you with your challenge or decision?

⊙ Their messages may not offer a literal solution, but you will intuit and reconnect to resources within you that you can trust. You may experience strong feelings and emotions welling up in you and that's OK – let them in and receive them with grace and gratitude.

Seek diverse perspectives

In the timeless tale *The Wizard of Oz*, Dorothy encounters some unexpected allies on her journey who help her find her way home again. They too are trying to find their way, searching for wholeness. The Scarecrow is searching for brains, the Tin Man wants a heart, and the Cowardly Lion seeks courage. *The Wizard of Oz* is part of the canon of archetypal stories that help us recognise universal truths about ourselves and the human condition. When we can recognise our role in these stories, we can see it more clearly, identify with it and learn from it.

Women instinctively know that the help and support of others makes a positive difference, and that help will come if they ask. But to do this, they first have to believe that being able to ask for help is a sign of strength.

Your help may come in the form of unexpected allies, like Dorothy's companions. Alas, they won't magically appear. You have to seek them out. But you get to choose your wise ones. (Then again, sometimes they *do* appear as if by magic in your life, at just the right moment, as if they have chosen *you*.)

You can ask for help from a diverse body of peers and colleagues, inside your network close to home or far afield. You can initiate one-to-one conversations or gather your wise ones together for a meeting for support, ideas and perspectives when you face a challenge.

Your allies will help you to feel well-resourced so that you can make a decision and take action with greater clarity and courage.

Here's a magnificent tool for your 'Dorothy' moment – for gathering wise ones and asking for help.

WISE COUNCIL
EXERCISE[32]

⊕ Invite four or five colleagues across as diverse a spread of sectors as possible to an hour-long meeting. You can always offer reciprocity of some sort.

⊕ Sit in a closed circle. Not around a table. Share your challenge story with your colleagues for a couple of minutes. Be as clear as possible. Share everything that is vital for them to know and how you're feeling about it.

⊕ Rule 1: No questions allowed. Your wise council of allies only listens.

⊕ After you've spoken, turn your chair around so that you're *sitting with your back to your group*. This is essential.

⊕ Your wise council now has ten to fifteen minutes to discuss your challenge and explore it from their perspectives. It's no longer your challenge. It's their challenge.

⊙ Rule 2: You are 'a fly on the wall' and cannot interrupt the discussion at any point. Just listen. Take notes if you wish.

⊙ At the end of their discussion, your wise council will invite you to turn your chair around and rejoin the group.

⊙ Rule 3: Give feedback to the group by saying something along these lines: 'Having heard your discussion, here's what's made an impact on me and here's an action I'm going to take...'

⊙ Rule 4: Keep your feedback short, specific, concise. Don't fall into a free-for-all conversation. Appreciate and thank your allies for their help and bring the meeting to an end.

By all means have a celebratory drink together if you'd like, but draw a line under the meeting before you socialise. You want to keep the strength and impact of your newly gathered resources close to you and not dissipate the energy of the learning before you've had a chance to reflect. You need the capacity to reflect on the resources that have been illuminated for you and on the action(s) you are committing to.

Mind the gaps in your network

If you've never created a network map, you're in for a revelatory gift. If you've made them before, chances are they're collecting dust and could use a review – you, too, are in for a revelatory gift.

A network map is a big drawing on a big piece of paper (you know the mantra; repeat after me: *work big*) using whatever symbols you wish to show your connections to people with whom you have relationships that help you in your growth, talent development and aspirations. There are countless examples online if you need inspiration.

It's useful to put actual names on your map and to show the nature of each relationship by using different symbols, colours, lines, etc. On your map, include those with whom you enjoy excellent, trusting, 'have your back' relationships, those you connect with frequently, those close by, those farther afield, those you need to connect with but have an unequal relationship with (or one that's more difficult to maintain) and so on. There's no right or wrong, but it's helpful to go big and spread the net as wide as possible.

When you're finished, take a step back and look over your map.

- What is revealed? What surprises you?

- How well is your current network serving your development, your goals and your vision?

- Is it cosy and comfortable?

- Is it diverse in gender? Is it generational? Does it spread across your organisation?

- Are there any glaring gaps in terms of what you need?

- To whom do you need to reach out? Why? When will you do that?

No matter how long it's been, people want to hear from you. If you're reaching for the stars, they'll make time for you. If they can't now, they will on another occasion. You're on their radar. Go and make those calls. Do it today.

Feedback improves performance

Just as a performer needs an audience you also need feedback. Knowing how to give it, how to receive it and what to do with it is vital; it's key to positive change and growth.

Think about a compliment you recently received from a friend or colleague and the 'feel good' glow you experienced in the moment. Now think about a negative or thoughtless remark someone made to you. Which experience are you still holding on to more? It's likely the negative remark affected you more deeply – maybe even consumed your thoughts for days!

The negativity bias refers to the tendency humans have to pay more attention, or give more weight, to negative experiences over positive ones. This is because in evolutionary terms, we're fighting or fleeing from predators. This basic survival radar is hardwired into us, even if we're no longer navigating around predators. This is exactly why we need to hit the fast-forward button in our personal evolution and build on more positive instincts.

Let's remove the character, *She who berates herself and dwells on the negative.* She's no longer needed in this story. Please exit stage left! Let's replace her with a new character.

Enter stage right! This character is *She who remains balanced and whole in the face of a disappointment, wound or sting.* She can reflect through the lens of her strengths and find affirmation. She can challenge, question, clear the air and move on. She is receptive but also discerning about the 'needs improvement' feedback she receives.

Feedback is a minefield. You say you want it, but how do you hear it and what do you do with it? Our responses to feedback – from 360 reviews to year-end appraisals, from performance reviews to the more casual, conversational moments of 'helpful observations' – are all too often mired in negativity. Dwelling on the negatives at the expense of the positives reinforces the myth that you're lacking something and need fixing.

Truly hearing and valuing the positive feedback you receive builds your forward momentum and gives you the confidence to use feedback as it has meaning and relevance for you.

Lauren, a bright, creative go-getter in a global accountancy firm, wanted to discuss the results of her 360 review. First, I summarised the outstandingly positive feedback regarding her strengths, her impact, and her contributions to her team. Lauren listened and made no response other than an occasional half-laugh.

Next, we discussed the areas for improvement, which totalled only two points, contextualised around a specific moment and a specific person. From that moment, Lauren kept steering our discussion back to these two points, holding on to them for dear life.

I could practically see her knuckles turning white from the effort, and this was over the phone! I led our discussion back to the positive feedback and asked Lauren how she felt about it. It was clear she hadn't even heard this feedback, let alone received or processed it.

Radical-action alert! I asked Lauren to get into a relaxed position, take a deep breath, close her eyes and just listen. Once she was settled, I read the positive feedback to her, slowly and deliberately, framing each point with a pause, like a gilded frame around a valuable painting. When I finished reading, I requested that we end our call without any further discussion. I wanted the last note Lauren heard to be positive.

Six months later, Lauren and I had another conversation. The woman on the other end of the phone sounded strong and upbeat. Her energy was palpable. Over those six months, Lauren had acted on her goals, made a real impact on her organisation, led some creative initiatives and was being put forward for a major promotion. When I asked Lauren what had shifted for her since our 360-review discussion, she replied, 'Hearing my positive feedback read aloud to me and really listening. I heard it for the first time.'

Truly hearing the positive feedback allowed Lauren to use it as a *body of evidence* about when and how she was at her best. Further, she processed it as a *resource*, an *ally* with which to shift her story, upgrade her self-belief and move forward in her visibility and credibility.

In the packed schedules and time pressures of the workplace, your responses to feedback can be rushed through and habitualised towards focusing on what you see as negative. Remember, feedback is impressionistic, human and highly subjective. It is con-textual and often time-specific, relating to a particular time, place and scenario. It can reflect perceptions gathered over a range of experiences that suggest a pattern or theme in the way you're seen and heard.

Feedback is an opportunity for reflection and choice. It's not designed for wholesale acceptance and unfil-tered absorption. It's designed to be an empowering agent for positive change and growth. Empowerment requires questions. Again, you don't need fixing; you are not lacking. You are a work in progress.

Always pay attention to positive feedback. Not only does it contribute to your strength-building story, it's also a practical resource for improvement. The more you understand your 'at your best' strengths, the more successfully you can apply them to your challenging scenarios with positive results. But none of this can happen unless you *hear, acknowledge, receive and value* your positive feedback.

Reflection is revealing

I recently came across an article outlining a potted history of London's Millennium Dome, that iconic exhibition space built to celebrate the beginning of the third millennium. I remember the huge controversy and long-running debate about what to put in the Dome once this vast and expensive site was created.

The proposal that won my vote was to leave the Dome empty as a futuristic temple of silence in the dawn of a new century already overwhelmed by sound pollution.

Not only did that not happen, the Dome eventually became a satellite of the O2 Centre, host of supersized pop music concerts with galactic sound systems and screaming fans. I still love the idea of the Dome as this enormous, intentional space, a kind of 'silence conservation' park.

When learning groups pause to reflect and write in their journals, the shared silence creates a uniquely beautiful and potent energy in the room. After this sense-making, people are more connected to themselves and to each other. There is a feeling of conscious valuing and meaning in the atmosphere where before there was a tendency to rush past things, experiencing – as T.S. Eliot notes in *Four Quartets* – without realising meaning.

You don't always have to ask for help externally. Asking for help by going inwards, to the place where you contemplate things, your breathing space, can quietly surprise. The practice of reflection and journaling helps us to sense-make, to process our thoughts and synthesise our learning. It's one of the most profoundly nurturing and self-helping practices I know. Your journal can include reflections on things you've learned, on things that went well in your day, on goals and actions, on things that inspire – the practice is uniquely yours. There are no rules, only the exploration of what this can bring.

I love the idea of keeping a 'best thing' journal. Asking yourself, 'What's the best thing that happened today?' might surface things you wouldn't ordinarily think about. If you ask yourself, 'What happened today?' it's likely you're going to remember something negative. The 'best thing' question gives you those fresh eyes of wonder – the girl awakened again.[33]

COACH IN YOUR POCKET POINTERS

- ⊕ Acknowledge positive feedback.

- ⊕ Harness diverse perspectives for help with your challenges.

- ⊕ Review your network and make a new connection.

- ⊕ Use reflection and journaling for awareness, feedback and self-coaching.

CHAPTER 9

Banish Size Zero
And Upsize
Your Visibility

*If no one answers the
phone, dial louder.*[34]

(LUCY, *PEANUTS*)

I'm browsing in one of those designer boutiques in a US airport – the kind with eye-watering price tags, even during the '50% off' sale. The impeccably groomed saleswoman is giving me a dubious once-over as she registers my 'functional' attire: trainers, jeans and a fleece.

There's one other customer in the boutique, a woman asking for a size zero in a dress on the rack containing what looks to me like dolls' clothes. The unbridled relief and triumph on this woman's face as the dress in size zero is produced fascinates me.

Why would anyone want to be a size zero and why has the fashion industry produced a size zero? What's wrong with extra small? Please understand, I'm not castigating women who are thin, svelte, lean, petite or any other shape or figure! I'm not talking about body weight at all. I'm talking about *language* and how it shapes our thinking.

'Size zero' conjures up 'size nothing', and why would any woman want to be a size nothing? Invisible? There's a cultural mindset that approves the idea of a size zero for women, and cultural norms influence *all* our thinking. It's easy to get ensnared in the net of assumptions they create, no matter how hard we try to forge our own path. No amount of Dove commercials or body-positivity campaigns can have meaning until the industry casts this absurd label into oblivion. Who are you serving by diminishing yourself?

Be your own talent scout

It's an old Hollywood myth. A talent scout notices a captivating woman sitting at the counter in a diner drinking her milkshake. He (it was always a 'he' in those days) sidles up to her and says the famous words: 'Kid, I'm gonna make you a star.' Those days are over, if they ever existed, and anyway, we're now in the #MeToo era so no one in their right mind would dare sidle up! The 'discovery' fairy tale is dead, and in its place a new story dawns. The woman at the soda fountain drinking her milkshake is also reading scripts, busy setting up her own production company and consulting her lawyers on the phone about her IP rights. She's bringing it on and manifesting her vision.

Meanwhile, in the workplace, you, too, have to replace the story that doing a great job will get you the recognition, credit or promotion you deserve. It's time to get noticed more and shine more. It's time to speak up. It's time to think up and feel taller, even without the stilettos. It's time to feel big on the inside. It's time to step into your fullest self and upsize your visibility. Having visibility enables you to inspire and galvanise others to support you and help you achieve your goals. Having visibility means having gravitas. It means that the message you transmit to your company is 'I'm ready'. It means having self-confidence and presence. It means using full stops at the end of your sentences to stand behind your words, and not ending your sentences in question marks, sounding tentative. Having visibility means enjoying the warmth of the spotlight rather than fearing its glare.

It means knowing your value, your unique strengths and gifts. It means initiating conversations and making connections. It means having a brand, a vision and a story you can communicate in as many ways as possible. Most importantly, your visibility is the difference between saying 'I' and hiding behind 'we'.

Claim the 'I'

Almost every time I ask a client to tell me about a positive result delivered, an achievement story or a significant contribution made, I have to stop the storyteller in her tracks, maybe three or four times, because there isn't an 'I' in sight. That stealthy little 'we' loves grabbing the spotlight! The generic 'we' is so dull. The specific 'I' is so compelling! Whose story is it anyway, if not yours?

Minimising your contribution or even putting yourself down to ensure you stay 'part of the team' is a misguided approach. You're squandering an opportunity to get your story right for those who need to hear it.

The great news is that you can 'claim the I' while also acknowledging others. It's not an either/or situation. There are times when you can have your cake and eat it too! To cross the threshold from the 'we' habit to the 'I' habit, here's something fun to try. You can work with a buddy or do this on your own, but you might want to close the door! You're going to work big and use the exaggeration tool you encountered in the rehearsal room in Chapter 7.

CLAIM THE 'I' EXERCISE

Stand up (get your whole body into this) and tell your 'I did it!' story. 'Act as if' you're one big self-enamoured narcissist. Go wild. Go over the top. Step into your diva persona and enjoy the biggest case of 'me-itis' you've ever had! Claim the 'I' and shout it from the rooftops. Blow your horn loud and clear. You're just playing. You can do it!

Think Miranda Priestly, that pathologically demanding editor in the film *The Devil Wears Prada*, played by Meryl Streep.

Or think like the goddess Aphrodite, gushing with self-adulation to one of her goddess pals in the firmament and ending on a flourish of fake-laugh humility, *Well, enough about me!*

Playing the exaggeration game requires nothing less than total embodiment – voice, physicality, gestures and laughter. That 'physical thinking' helps rewire your brain and replace the 'we' crutch with the 'I' platform. So say it loud and proud.

Emphasise the word 'I' every time you say it, with as much force and exaggeration and spotlight-grabbing intention as possible. Make any gestures you want to seal the deal, steal the show and make your imprint.

Now that you've gone way over the top with the 'I', tell your story again and see where you can acknowledge the 'we'. Keep it relevant but sparse. Keep it gracious but keep it moving. Be sure to end on the 'I' note.

It's essential that you understand that claiming the 'I' isn't arrogance but valuing; not selfishness but ownership; not basking in the spotlight but shining your light so others can see. Having the gravitas, presence and integrity to be able to claim the 'I' and also credit and appreciate others is key to your visibility. If you don't claim your 'I', someone else will.

Your personal brand

Imagine you're having your yearly eye test. You look through the lenses as the optician turns them this way and that to test strengths and image sharpness. Due to some technical breakdown or momentary blip into a parallel universe of oddities, instead of seeing letters and numbers, what you see on the screen are partial logos of consumer-product brands.

Even though you see only mere fragments of logos, your brand recognition powers are mighty. Apple! Nescafé! Louis Vuitton! Mercedes! Nike! Coca-Cola! Perrier! and so on and so on. You call out each one, undaunted and invincible. So strong is your brand recognition acumen you need only the slightest hint of the logos, a few dots of colour, a shape and an accent, to recognise each product. Your optician is impressed.[35] Why are brands so powerful? Because we have an emotional relationship with them. They stand out amongst all the competing noise. The brands we choose serve us consistently and we trust them.

According to a study on conscious consumerism, most shoppers are now considered to be 'belief-driven' buyers. Here are some of the key qualities that are considered most attractive in a brand:

- Delivering on promises

- Transparency

- Treating employees well

- Having ethical values and authenticity

- Passion

- Belief

- Taking a stance on issues close to the buyer's heart[36]

You are not a commercial product, but you do stand for something. You have values, vision, competencies, outstanding strengths and unique contributions that you can bring to the table. Your brand works as a symbol for the 'You Portfolio', and there are times you need to sell yourself so that you're seen and heard by the people who need to know.

The subject of personal branding is a popular one, and there are loads of books and articles out there to help you. It's a vital part of your performance because as we've seen, doing a good job won't in itself get you a seat at the table.

Here are some things to think about when creating your brand:

- What are you the 'go to' person for?

- What capabilities are you known for?

- Why do people trust you?

- How do you create that trust?

- What are your core values?

- How do you exercise these values, especially under pressure or when challenged?

- In a few words, how would your colleagues and friends describe you?

- Why are you a great fit for a particular role?

- What are the unique qualities you bring to what you do?

- What do you feel passionate about and how do you communicate that?

BRAND QUALITIES EXERCISE

⊕ Share a success story with a trusted friend or colleague – a time when you were highly effective and at your best. This can be the same 'at your best' story you told in the Chapter 5 exercise or a completely new one. You've had loads of successes.

⊕ *Write down* all the feedback from your listener about the qualities, characteristics and attributes they get about you from hearing your 'at your best' story. Thank them for their feedback. This part is really important! They are giving you a gift.

⊕ Look at your feedback and circle words that leap out at you. They might attract you energetically or feel true, or maybe you just like the sound of them. Don't overthink it – go with your gut.

⊕ Now choose three words (this will be a big 'commit moment' if you've circled lots of them!) and write them on a fresh piece of paper. Write your list on a *big, epic, bold* scale. Think billboard.

⊕ Stand up and say aloud, 'When I'm at my best, I am WORD 1, WORD 2 and WORD 3.'

> ⊙ Notice what you feel emotionally, energetically
>   and physically as you speak each word.
>   Practise saying this short statement until your
>   partner believes you, or, if you're doing this on
>   your own, until you believe yourself.
>
> ⊙ Get interested in the differences between each
>   word. Consider their sounds and meaning for
>   you. Feel as if you're planting those three flags
>   in the ground with force or holding up those
>   three billboards that 'announce' you. These
>   powerful words are gateways to the story of
>   your impact when you upsize your visibility.

Communicate your vision

A visitor walks through a town in medieval Italy and happens upon a man cutting stone. The visitor asks, 'What are you doing?' The man says he is cutting stone. The visitor continues and sees another man cutting stone. The visitor asks the same question, and this man replies, 'I'm building a wall.' A while later, the visitor encounters a third man cutting stone, and when he asks this man what he's doing, the man says, 'I'm building a cathedral.'[37]

Knowing your immediate job is one thing; knowing the part you play in the bigger picture, and what you want to create, is another – this is your vision. When you have a vision, you imagine a future state beyond boundaries. Identifying and communicating a clear vision is key to your visibility. The very word *vision* relates to seeing, and we often think of the words attributed to Aristotle, that 'The soul never thinks without a picture.'

The realm of the visual releases in you new ways of seeing, and this surfaces fresh, out-of-the ordinary language. Images engage your senses and intuition. In the prologue to Shakespeare's *Henry V*, the narrator invites the audience to use their imaginations to transform a paltry stage and a few ragtag players into the epic battlefield at Agincourt. 'Think, when we talk of horses, that you see them printing their proud hooves in the receiving earth.'[38] The narrator beckons and enchants the audience to share in a vision and see through their imaginations with the help of his word pictures.

Images 'say' things to you without your needing to analyse or overthink them. Visualising, painting pictures in words, creating a vision board and dedicating some time to consciously 'looking' in nature, in art galleries, and all around you will ignite your creative flow and help you access and craft your vision.

An organisation in the auto industry once launched a storytelling campaign to share their vision and get everyone in the organisation on board. Huge portraits of the employees and text that conveyed their part in the organisational story filled the gallery space and created an immersive experience. Everyone had a sense of being part of something bigger than themselves and something they could all see and feel proud of.

Your vision isn't simply a well-crafted statement that you write down. It's alive in you. It's your North Star, clarifying what your achievement will look like and how to get there.

When Alice asks the Cheshire Cat, 'Would you tell me, please, which way I ought to go from here?', the cat says, 'That depends a good deal on where you want to get to.'[39] A beautifully apt response.

Having a vision helps you set your compass to what really matters to you and what you want to focus on. It is a living, energising story that transcends the status quo and galvanises you towards a future you want to create.

It's critical to share your vision with others. Part of upsizing your visibility involves communicating your vision in as many ways as possible to everyone who needs to hear it. For this to happen, you need to aim for bold, big and simple.

Amanda Steinberg, CEO of DailyWorth, started with the belief that 'financially empowered women are the key to world peace'. From that belief came her well-known statement, 'I want to use my gifts of intelligence, charisma and serial optimism to cultivate the self-worth and net-worth of women around the world'[40].

Talk about claiming the 'I' and valuing her strengths in service to others!

There are a lot of semantics around what makes a mission statement and what makes a vision statement. Steinberg's is a blend of both and galactic in its reach. Like it or loathe it, it's a statement that illustrates thinking big, making it personal and being bold.

Here's my vision statement at the moment: I want to unlock the extraordinary potential of every talented, aspiring woman I coach. I believe that leveraging their visibility, values and voices will create healthier organisations and more enlightened leadership in the world.

You want to inspire yourself and others with your vision. You want to attract commitment to your vision. You want nothing less than to be the Pied Piper of visibility with your vision! OK. It's time to start crafting your vision statement.

McKinsey's master expert in leadership, Johanne Lavoie, introduced me to this visualisation exercise during the *Centered Leadership* programme at the Banff Centre, in Canada. It's a beautiful way to kick-start the process.

VISION EXERCISE

- ⊕ Take time out to stop. Now sit or lie down, relax, close your eyes and breathe deeply, luxuriously.

- ⊕ Visualise yourself in a moment of peak performance, a moment when you were energised, passionate, effective, in flow, connected to your belief and purpose, making a difference.

- ⊕ Ask yourself: 'When I am in this state (list all the words that describe you in this state), what am I able to create?'

- ⊕ Use your response to craft a short vision statement.

- ⊕ Practise speaking your vision statement with an *energetic launching phrase*. For example, 'What inspires me is... '; 'Picture this... '; 'I see... '; 'I believe that... ' An energetic launching phrase points you forward and gives you lift off, so you can speak with traction, confidence and belief.

If you're grappling with crafting your vision and drawing a blank, don't panic. There's no deadline other than 'Begin'! Keep the process open and ongoing. Here's a creative exploration tool from the rehearsal room that you might enjoy. It's an improvisation for two called 'Yes, and...', and it might just release some vision triggers for you!

YES, AND... IMAGINATION FLOW EXERCISE

- ⊕ You will need a partner and a timer. Set for two minutes (your timer, not your partner!).

- ⊕ Stand face-to-face.

- ⊕ Propose to your partner an idea or first thought about something you want to do, create or envision. It can be realistic or completely fictional. This is an improvisation exercise, so remember, you're playing! For example, 'Would you like to take a hot air balloon ride and crack open a bottle of champagne on the way?' could be your opening proposal. Or you could keep it real: 'Will you join me in organising a company marathon to raise money for my girls-to-leaders project?' Get the idea?

- ⊕ Your partner can respond *only* with 'Yes, and...'. They must build on your proposition.

- ⊕ You *must* reply to your partner starting with 'Yes, and...'. Keep building on each other's responses and keep the volley going fast: no pauses, no stops, no thinking – just instinct.

- ⊕ When you're done, summarise the wild card scenario you conjured up together.

During that improvisational dialogue, notice your energy levels and your physical and vocal animation. Notice how it feels to receive, accept and build on ideas with a 'yes' state of mind. Notice what happens when you have to keep going *no matter what* and what happens when you have to work fast, *without preparation*, and just dive in.

Like visual images, this kind of free-associating and riffing on a start point liberates your thinking into that dream space you know as blue-sky thinking. Somewhere in that 'wild, anything is possible' scenario, there will be a gem, a gold nugget of an idea that glistens and catches your attention.

There will be a feeling, an emotion and a powerful truth from your inner voice. It might be an 'aha' moment; it might be the quiet beginning of something about to unfold. Your vision is already in the making.

Who knows?

You're doing a great job as a committed, accountable, talented professional.

You deliver what you're tasked with. You perform. You've got a personal brand and a vision. You make a positive impact on those around you and think about how you're seen and heard. You have impact.

So, who knows about you and what you can contribute? Who needs to know? How are you communicating, broadcasting and promoting the story of your great performance? How are you leveraging your impact? What is your exposure-barometer reading?

Let's go back to basics for a moment. Now is a great time to revisit your elevator pitch – that short but compelling introduction of yourself that's always at the ready. It's the story of who you are, what you do and what you're so ready to do next. It's bold, simple, clear and specific. It's dynamic and energised. Any time a key stakeholder, panel interviewer or potential champion asks you 'What do you do?' or 'How do you see your fit for this role?' or you find yourself in any of those 'Who are you and what do I need to know?' moments, make yourself visible through your elevator pitch. This is a 'claim the I' moment!

Enjoy revisiting, revising or creating a fit-for-purpose elevator pitch. Stay away from work jargon and keep it real! Here are some points to include:

- Your name and your job title and what that really means. What's the story behind your title?

- What energises and excites you about your role?

- What are your key strengths?

- What is the impact you want to have on the organisation? What do you want to contribute?

Try creating a bullet-point version of this story and speak it out loud to get a shape and flow that sounds natural and utterly convincing. You can tell this story in less than a minute, or even in a couple of sentences, trust me, and the more familiar you are with your story, the more you can flex it for any situation as you need it.

Your virtual visibility (I'm googling you right now)

According to research from the Cranfield School of Management, 78% of professionals looking for information on new colleagues or prospective hires search online first.[41]

If I googled you right now, or looked you up on LinkedIn, what would I find? Don't forget about your virtual visibility across your organisation. Pay attention to what you communicate in your online profiles. Virtual environments are the phenomenon of our time, and the ability to leverage them is one of the greatest resources you can have when it comes to upsizing your visibility.

COACH IN YOUR POCKET POINTERS

- Practise claiming the 'I' when you communicate your contributions and achievements.

- Hone your personal introduction or elevator pitch so it's fit for multiple purposes.

- Craft a vision statement, practise speaking it and get feedback on its impact.

- Do a personal-brand audit.

- Maintain your virtual visibility.

CHAPTER 10

Summon Your Inner Revolutionary

*I am no longer accepting the
things I cannot change.
I am changing the things
I cannot accept.*

(ANGELA DAVIS)

In the wake of events celebrating the women's vote centenary, I enjoyed an opportunity to choreograph a new play called *The Cause*. It's about suffrage leaders Emmeline Pankhurst and Millicent Fawcett.[42]

Although fighting for the same cause, these two women represented very different voices and strategies. Pankhurst was a militant activist (deeds not words) who engaged in acts of civil disobedience and destruction and spent years enduring prison and force-feeding. Fawcett campaigned via socially and politically peaceful means (diplomacy, dialogue, non-violence) and led an altogether more genteel and secure life, but was equally committed to creating change. These extraordinary women with their utterly authentic voices and values were revolutionaries whose legacies live on and continue to shape every aspect of life for women today.

It's inspiring to visualise your personal procession of revolutionary women through time. I see Isadora Duncan, liberator of the female dancer from tutus, pointe shoes and idealised ephemerality to earthy, barefoot, tunic-flowing dance maker. I see Coco Chanel, transformer of female fashion from oppressive corsets and bustles to the functional, pared down chic of jackets and trousers. The list marches on.

We all have heroines who inspire awe, gratitude and humility in us. After all, their legacies changed mindsets and cultural norms. They awakened their audiences and the world with 'the shock of the new'. They forever changed the status quo.

Our revolutionaries had big visions and irrepressible spirits. They didn't retreat from the phrase 'This can't be done', didn't collapse in the face of 'No'. They persevered. They often suffered and failed. They attracted advocates, fans and admirers. They started riots. They carried on their paths. They believed in their visions.

We do indeed stand on the shoulders of giantesses, and they are transformative role models of *the possible*. That said, you don't need to be epic and iconic to be a revolutionary. Within you is your own revolutionary, poised for acts of courage, risk-taking, standing up and being counted, speaking up, initiating, and stretching – whatever these acts may be for you. Perhaps:

- Speaking first in the meeting where you've always held back

- Making that presentation to more senior, knowledgeable colleagues and believing in your value

- Taking a visible stand on an issue that's important to you

- Calling something out when you see it, such as an unconscious bias in operation

Within you is your own revolutionary who wants to change the story of 'living in an epidemic of obedience',[43] as Nancy Kline put it, and who will dare to do something differently for herself and others. Dress outside the unspoken company conventions; own your ethnicity, your differences, your *otherness* in a more visible way; help initiate better conversations about diversity; create something you'd love to see in your workplace – start a choir or book club, or take the lead on getting a company crèche set up.

Remember that your iconic revolutionaries were singularly dedicated to their causes. Their missions were all-consuming. They were tireless, driven, obsessed and ferociously uncompromising. They took enormous risks.

Embracing your inner revolutionary might not feel quite so perilous, so enjoy the breathing space of experimentation! Like my Irish friends say, 'You can be a legend in your own lunchtime.'

Take a moment to reflect on a risk or action you'd like to take, or a stretch you'd like to make. Just as you did when crafting your vision and imagining what it would look like, envision the step your inner revolutionary wants to take. Ask yourself: What will be the consequences of *not* doing this?

There are so many things you can do to move forward with courage and creativity, as your fullest and most authentic self. Drop the corporate mask; allow yourself to express emotion rather than damping it down;

share your vulnerability rather than blockading it; speak language that conveys your meaning effectively rather than speaking in the shorthand company jargon; harness your animated, passionate, energised self and don't let it atrophy under conformity and conventions that may be long out of date. You have everything you need.

- You have your faithful ally *Stop! and breathe.*

- You have the reawakened girl within – your reclaimed passion, imagination, sense of wonder and playfulness.

- You value your stories for yourself and in service to others.

- You stand tall, set clear intentions, and create maximum engagement with your presence.

- You prepare *yourself*, not just your content.

- You ask, 'What's needed here?' for impact and influence.

- You use your whole energy wardrobe.

- You're great at *how* you say what you say because you've *tuned up* how you *turn up.*

- You rehearse to stay fresh and grow your creativity.

- Your brand and vision are in progress and you are increasingly fluent in communicating them.

- You are 'unstoppable but willing to pivot'[44] because you are focused as well as flexible.

- You have the strength and wisdom to ask for help and build your network.

- You have the gravitas to 'claim the I' and to shine your light on others, too.

- You have an inner coach, and her voice is louder than your inner critic's.

When you summon your inner revolutionary, you can create your own template for leadership and help change the story of what professional life looks like.

Nothing short of expressing your inner revolutionary is needed to create the change you want to see in the workplace – to create a workplace where you and your integrated life and work, your *lifework* can thrive.

My personal motivational lifeline for exercising my own inner revolutionary is witnessing inspirational performances by great performers. When I jump up from my seat to give a standing ovation I see the world differently and every strand of my being feels so very alive. Memorable performances by outstanding performers make me feel I have hit a new key in the song of my life. I feel 'more' in every way: more awake; more hopeful; more resolved; more courageous; more optimistic; more passionate; and more galvanised.

This is what happens when you, like great performers, fully commit to your gifts. When you step into your fullest, fearless authenticity you inspire, ignite, and make a difference. Your inner revolutionary awakens.

The call of the revolutionary within you, whether gentle or gigantic, silent or seismic, diplomatic or disruptive, is your unique energy and gift that must be expressed. As Martha Graham reminds us:

> There is a vitality, a life force, an energy, a
> quickening, that is translated through you
> into action, and because there is only one of
> you in all time, this expression is unique. And
> if you block it, it will never exist through any
> other medium and it will be lost.[45]

The greatest act of your inner revolutionary is the act of bringing yourself fully through that door and performing as *you* in all the roles you play. Go forth. The world needs you.

References

1. J. Brown, 'Fire', *The Art and Spirit of Leadership* (Trafford Publishing, 2012), p147.

2. Jennifer Cohen and Jason Gore, 'Somatic Practice: A Path to Mastery for 21st Century Leaders', *The Mobius Strip* (Mobius Executive Leadership, August 2013), p4.

3. Jim Loehr and Tony Schwartz, 'The Making of a Corporate Athlete', *Harvard Business Review* (Harvard Business Publishing January 2001), p122.

4. I learned the 'candle blowing' breath exercise from my colleague Didi Hopkins at Theatre 4 Business.

5. Walt Whitman, 'Song of the Open Road', *Leaves of Grass*, first published 1855, verse 5, lines 8-9.

6. Austin Kleon, Steal Like an Artist (Workman Publishing Company, 2012), p54.

7. Amy Cuddy, 'Your Body Language May Shape Who You Are' (TEDGlobal, June 2012), 15.24.

8. William Shakespeare, Hamlet, Act 1, Scene 2 (first soliloquy).

9. Milhaly Csikszentmihalyi, *Flow: The Psychology of Happiness* (Harper Perennial Modern Classics, 2008). The concept of flow is explored and defined throughout this seminal work.

10. Walt Whitman, 'Song of Myself', *Leaves of Grass*, first published 1855, verse 51, line 9.

11. Rebecca Solnit, *The Faraway Nearby* (Granta Publications, 2013), p3.

12. Franz Kafka, 'Letter to Oskar Pollak, 1904', *Letters to Friends, Families and Editors* (Schocken, 1990), p16.

13. Walt Whitman, 'Song of the Open Road', *Leaves of Grass*, first published 1855, verse 10, last line.

14. Gloria Swanson as character Norma Desmond in the film *Sunset Boulevard* (Paramount Pictures 1950).

15. Amy Cuddy, 'Julianne Moore Interview' *Presence, Bringing Your Boldest Self to your Biggest Challanges* (Orion Books, 2016), p64.

16. Anica Louw, Shawbrook Dance, County Longford, Ireland.

17. Michael McIntyre sketch, 'When You Don't Hear Someone', Facebook Group: Michael McIntyre Fans (2017) 26 July. Available at: www.facebook.com/MichaelMcIntyreFans/videos/when-you-dont-hear-someone-/1441735499181197/ (Accessed: May 7, 2017).

18. Amy Cuddy, *Presence: Bringing your boldest self to your biggest challenges* (Orion Books, 2016), p215.

19. Nely Galán, *Self Made* (Spiegel & Grau, 2016), p97.

20. Facebook: M. Angelou@Mayaangelou (2013) 30 January. Available at: www.facebook.com/MayaAngelou/posts/stand-up-straight-and-realize-who-you-are-that-you-tower-over-your-circumstanc es/10151477761954796/ (Accessed: February 3, 2019).

21. Lewis Carroll, *Alice's Adventures in Wonderland and Through the Looking-Glass* (Oxford University Press, 2008), p40.

22. 'Facebook's Mark Zuckerberg: Why I wear the same T-shirt every day', *The Telegraph* online edition (2014) 7 November. Available at: www.telegraph.co.uk/technology/facebook/11217273/Facebooks-Mark-Zuckerberg-Why-I-wear-the-same-T-shirt-every-day.html (Accessed: December 3, 2018).

23. Maya Angelou, *The Guardian* online edition (2014) 29 May. Available at: www.theguardian.com/books/2014/may/28/maya-angelou-in-fifteen-quotes (Accessed: January 3, 2017).

24. Cited in Max A. Eggert, *Body Language Pocket Book* (Management Pocket Books, 2012), p17.

25. Eileen McDargh, Keynote Speech: 'Radical Resiliency: A Key to Disrupting the Ordinary', (International Simmons Leadership Conference, Dublin, 2018).

26. theatertalk, 'Theater Talk Legendary Lyricist Sheldon Harnick', YouTube (20 May 2011), www.youtube.com/watch?v=vufxoUQPNOs (Accessed: February 5, 2019).

27. Pina Bausch, Speech (Kyoto Prize Award Ceremony, Kyoto, Japan 2007), published courtesy of the Inamori Foundation.

28. Pierre Jourdan, *I Am A Dancer* (UK, 1972).

29. Samuel Beckett, *Worstward Ho* (Calder Publications, 1983).

30. Martha Graham, *Blood Memory: An Autobiography* (Doubleday, 1991).

31. Hillary Rodham Clinton, *It Takes a Village* (Simon & Schuster UK, 2007).

32. I learned this exercise from my colleague and collaborator Josie Sutcliffe, Theatre 4 Business.

33. Nicholson Baker's advice to keep a journal of 'the best thing that happened to me today', cited in Austin Kleon, *Steal Like an Artist* (Workman Publishing Company, 2012), p130.

34. Lucy, *Peanuts*, Charles Shultz.

35. The partial logos story is based on a slide deck about brand, created by Boardwalk Leadership and More2Gain, for a women's leadership programme I collaborated on for Akzo Nobel in 2015.

36. Raconteur, 'The Future of Retail', *The Sunday Times*, 7 March, 2019.

37. 'Building A Vision' (Leading For Results programme, The Banff Centre), based on John Baldoni, *How Great Leaders Get Great Results* (Mcgraw-Hill Education, 2006).

38. William Shakespeare, Henry V, Act 1, Prologue.

39. Lewis Carroll, *Alice's Adventures in Wonderland and Through the Looking-Glass* (Oxford University Press, 2008), p57.

40. Drew Hendricks, Personal Mission Statements of 13 CEOs and Lessons You Need to Learn, *Forbes* online (2014) 10 November. Available at: www.forbes.com/sites/drewhendricks/2014/11/10/personal-mission-statement-of-14-ceos-and-lessons-you-need-to-learn/#6b58af61e5ea (Accessed: September 22, 2016).

41. Research presentation by Cranfield for HOST: Accelerating for Difference Programme, HSBC, 14-16 February 2017.

42. Natalie McGrath, *The Cause – An Overture of Rebellion and Revolt* (Methuen, 2018). Production directed by Josie Sutcliffe, Dreadnought SW; toured the UK in 2018.

43. Nancy Kline, *More Time to Think: The Power of Independent Thinking* (Cassell, 2015), p15.

44. Halla Tómasdóttir, Keynote Speech: 'Be a Change Catalyst: Lessons for Principled Leadership', (International Simmons Leadership Conference, Dublin, 2018).

45. Martha Graham, in a letter to Agnes de Mille, *Dance to the Piper & Promenade Home* (Da Capo Press, 1982).

Acknowledgements

I feel very blessed to have so many thanks to express.

I am deeply grateful to all the amazing women (and men!) I get to coach. I really believe I have the best job on the planet.

A special thanks to the fantastic team at Rethink Press, Roger Waltham, Eve Makepeace, Anke Ueberberg, Lucy McCarraher and Joe Gregory who made such a difference.

Theatre 4 Business, the platform that has shaped so much of my work, was co-founded with my long-time collaborator Josie Sutcliffe, along with Mary Lidgate and Didi Hopkins. All we knew at the time, seventeen years ago, was that there was something incredible to be explored in the meeting ground between the arts and business. All of us came from theatre backgrounds and all of us believed that theatre offers a lens through which performance on the business stage can be experienced and leveraged for great results. These beliefs have strengthened through practice and evidence over the years.

My gratitude to Josie Sutcliffe is ongoing and profound. From our first encounter twenty years ago to our most recent work, we've been creative collaborators and friends, mutually igniting and inspiring and having each other's backs. This book began as a collaboration, springing from the deep, fertile ground of so many rich conversations we've had about theatre, coaching and leadership. We've enjoyed fantastically productive moments of dissonance and creative explosion. Consensus has always taken a back seat on our metaphorical road trips. Long may our sparks fly, Josie.

To Professor Sue Vinnicombe at Cranfield University, a huge thanks for your generous reading and review time of the final manuscript. To the women who committed time from their incredibly full days to give me their feedback when this book was in its draft stages, my gratitude shall hover around you like a friendly spirit always: Sarah Rayner, Kate Jones, Julianne Antrobus, Autumn Le Fevre, Jo Palmer, Sarah Fennell and Josefin Holmberg. Sarah, thanks also for saying you wish you could have me in your pocket as your coach, which inspired the idea for the Coach in Your Pocket Pointers at the end of each chapter. Josefin, on another note, hearing you sing so magnificently once upon a time, during a women's program, reawakened my lifelong yearning to sing. I'm happy to say I've been singing ever since, with love and thanks to the extraordinary voice coach Claude Stein. I truly believe there is a magical relationship between singing and writing. It certainly gave me more expression in both voices.

To the immensely creative and accomplished Didi Hopkins, my colleague and friend, many years of thanks for all that I've learned from your distinctive voice as a coach and artist. Alison Temperley, author of *Inside Knowledge: How Women Can Thrive in Professional Service Firms*, thank you for your support and encouragement, practical advice and proof-reading assistance. Marty Boroson, author of *The One Moment Master: Stillness for people on the go*, thanks for being my 'go to' resource for provocative conversations and asker of rigorous questions.

To Helen Chadwick and Rona Lee, beautiful artists and allies, my big thanks for all your input in our co-coaching circle. Liz Norris, in Dublin, thank you for inviting me into your space to share our practices, and for such uplifting discussions. To my friends in 'the gals writing group', Lily Susan Todd and Mary Lucas, deep thanks not only for endowing our group with such profound attention and love of language, but also for your steadfast encouragement to keep writing. To my dear friend Basia Irland, thanks for all your support and sanctuary when I started this journey and for being a constant source of inspiration.

To my former co-founders at Boardwalk Leadership, Lady (Kitty) Chisholm and Dr Shaheena Janjuha-Jivraj, incredibly smart women and authors of *Championing Women Leaders: Beyond Sponsorship*, my thanks to you is rooted in our special history as creative collaborators.

To grow your performance, you need opportunities to practise. Over the years, the Cranfield School of Management has given me a home in which to cultivate my voice and methodology. I thank all my very special colleagues there for your support and the great experience of working with you. Colin Funk introduced me to the Banff Centre over a decade ago and helped set my course for a long and rich association there. Johanne Lavoie, partner at McKinsey, Calgary, shared her Centered Leadership practice with me and introduced me to the transformational community Mobius Executive Leadership; I have gained so much from you both, thank you.

Cynthia Morris at Original Impulse is the inspiring coach who got me back to writing again after I'd repeated the same old story to myself too many times: 'I'd love to but I don't have the time, blah, blah, blah.' Thank you, Cynthia – you rock! Thanks to Mindy Gibbons-Klein, The Book Midwife who taught me invaluable processes about getting a book to the delivery room!

The biggest driver of this book was love. The love of my family gives me strength and joy every day.

My sons, Justin and Toban, and daughters-in-law, Kate and Ann, all *lean in* together and live and perform beautifully. They make life's endeavours meaningful for me. Cole, Paige, Leo, Ember and Ari most definitely keep the girl in me *awakened*!

My husband, Arno, gets top billing in my thanks. I can hear him say (Groucho-Marx style), 'So why am I at the bottom of the page?' My answer is 'Because it's the final thing I want everyone to remember.' Thank you for your steadfast love and support. You are my rock. And thank you for giving me the best room in the house for my office.

The Author

As Director of Theatre 4 Business, international performance coach, author, and speaker, **Diana Theodores** applies her years of experience in professional dance, theatre directing and writing on the arts to the principles of 'great performance' on the business stage. Her mission is to help people shine in every role they play in their organisations. Diana serves on the faculties of The Cranfield School of Management, The Banff Centre and Mobius Executive Leadership. She has been facilitating leadership, communications and presence programmes since 2005. Diana works with clients worldwide across diverse industries, from energy to entertainment, sports to finance, and retail to technology. Her dynamic and embodied approach has offered a transformational experience to thousands of women and men, connecting them with their unique voice, presence and authentic impact. She has a PhD from Trinity College, Dublin, and trained at the NLP and Coaching Institute of California. She is a native of New York and lives in London.

Contact Diana at:

🌐 www.theatre4business.com

in www.linkedin.com/in/d1ana

f www.facebook.com/theatre4business

🐦 @t4bshine

Made in the USA
Las Vegas, NV
29 April 2021

22196967R00122